This book is dedicated to the memory

of

Tony Waddington

The Long Hard Road

To

Wembley

The Long Hard Road To Wembley

33

of 300.

The Long Hard Road

To

Wembley

Andrew Hine

Man Mountain Publishing

Stoke on Trent

First published in Great Britain by
Man Mountain Publishing,
8 Easedale Close, Baddeley Green,
Stoke-on-Trent. Staffs. ST2 7PN.

ISBN 1 899003 83 5

Printed and bound by
Sovereign Bookcare, 28-30 Hartshill Road, Stoke on Trent, ST4 7QU

Foreword

The rain was coming down in sheets, the January wind bitterly cold against your face, it was typical Manchester weather! Even the weather didn't deter over 49,000 fans, the majority of them Stokies, from turning out for the game. And what a game - Moore in goal for the injured Ferguson, a penalty saved but not the follow-up. Then finally a TC goal to put Stoke 3-2 up.

We hung on for the last 30 minutes in the mud and rain, every Stokie in Old Trafford willing the impossible to happen. Eventually the final whistle went. Turning to my Dad, I screamed at the top of my voice - "We've done it Dad, we've done it, we're going to Wembley".

The waiting was over, the agony of Hillsborough was forgotten, and we, Stoke City, the club who had never won anything, were finally going to a major cup final. The long hard road to Wembley was complete.

As a young Potters fan, that night at Old Trafford is my abiding memory of the '72 League Cup campaign. Of course, at thirteen, you think that there will be lots more nights like that, little did I know how few there would actually be and how pleased I am now that I have such vivid memories of my heroes. Those heroes went on to not only win the League Cup, but also to form the basis of the team that drew twice with the mighty Ajax in the UEFA Cup and to challenge for the First Division (Premiership) title in '74/75. This was truly a great time to be a Stoke fan.

Thirty years later, March 2002, I was fortunate to be personally involved in the 30th anniversary celebrations and can tell you that all the players have the fondest memories of '72 and a great passion for Stoke City as a club.

Thanks to Andrew Hine's wonderful book, all of us, young or old, can revisit that triumphant Cup run through the eyes of those players. Thanks again Andrew, and if you are under thirty, that really was Chelsea, West Ham and Man. Utd. we were playing and beating!

Gooooaaarrrrn Stoke.

Phil Rawlins
Director.
Stoke City F.C.

The Long Hard Road To Wembley

We've Won The Cup

On March 4th 1972 at about 5.15 p.m. an epic adventure reached its glorious conclusion as Stoke City Football Club, the 'Pride of the Potteries', ended a 108-year wait by beating the playboys of the Kings Road (Chelsea) to win the Football League Cup 2-1. Not only was it the climax of a wait of epic proportions for the club's first trophy but it was also the victorious culmination of an heroic and extended cup run.

This book has been written, not only to recall that momentous cup run, which started at lowly Southport's Haig Avenue and finished beneath the famous 'Twin Towers' of Wembley Stadium, it also remembers those players and officials of Stoke City who brought a major trophy back to the Potteries for the first time ever.

Just like a football match, this is a book of two halves. The first half recalls and recounts the action that took place during that amazing adventure, remembering what happened as the players journeyed from Southport to Wembley via Oxford, Manchester, Bristol and the extended semi-final games. The second half pays tribute to our heroes who wore the red and white stripes so valiantly, recalling such moments as Gordon's famous penalty save and T.C's goal in the final amongst others.

As with any match there is usually time added on by the referee, likewise, with this book there is an extra chapter which pays tribute to our opponents that day, Chelsea.

We therefore hope that you will find this book both informative and entertaining.

From Southport To Wembley

Oh, I Do Like To Be Beside The Seaside.

Stoke City's 1971-72 League Cup adventure started with a visit to 4th division Southport's seaside home of Haig Avenue on Wednesday 8th September.

There was an air of determination surrounding the Stoke players as they purposefully ran out onto the pitch, despite a very late change to their team, as 'keeper Gordon Banks, who had earlier been cleared to play following a bout of influenza, came down with an ear infection ruling him out from the starting line-up and was replaced by John Farmer, the former England under 23 international. John Mahoney was also drafted into the side, replacing Terry Conroy in the number seven shirt. Teams:

Southport: - Taylor, Turner, Sibbald, McPhee, Dunleavey, Peat, Lee, Hartland, Redrobe, Field, Hartle. substitute, Lloyd.

Stoke City: - Farmer, Marsh, Pejic, Bernard, Smith, Bloor, Mahoney, Greenhoff, Ritchie, Dobing, Haslegrave. substitute, Stevenson.

Spurred on by their largest crowd of the season, 10,223, Southport started the game in such a style as to belie their lowly league status. Southport's Field was proving to be a handful during the opening exchanges, beating both Bloor and Pejic in a bustling run that was only brought to a halt by midfield hardman, Mike Bernard. Field was then involved in the first real chance of the game when he met a cross with a well-directed header which, fortunately for the 'Potters', bounced clear off the crossbar.

In the tenth minute, defender **Alan Bloor** brought the ball away from the Stoke penalty area and, crossing the half-way line, played a one-two with striker Jimmy Greenhoff. Regaining the ball, he was hurried into attempting a speculative left-foot shot which flew past the Southport 'keeper Taylor, skidding just inside the left-hand post for the first goal.

Pic. E. Fuller

Southport broke back from a long goalkick which Redrobe latched onto, charging forward he blasted the ball goal-ward but John Farmer earned his

This chapter has been kindly supported by Carl W. Holness.

match bonus with that save alone, managing a full-length dive, to push the ball around the post for a corner.

Pic. E. Fuller

Southport continued to play well above their standard, constantly pressurising the Stoke goal. In the sixteenth minute, Dunleavey, the former Evertonian, advanced into the penalty area forcing another Southport corner. Field un-sighted the Stoke 'keeper as he mistimed his leap, leaving the ball to continue its trajectory, only to be re-directed into the net by **Dunleavey**, despite what appeared to be a foul upon the Stoke 'keeper. Regardless of the Stoke players' protestations which were led by John Ritchie, referee Harold Hackney allowed the goal, booking the big forward for good measure.

Stoke City continued to press forward as the half wore on, when Jimmy Greenhoff, breaking across the penalty area, fired a point blank shot at the target. Southport's 'keeper Taylor made a

'Jenningsesque' save as the ball rebounded off his legs for a corner.

The most dramatic moment of the first-half occurred in the 35th minute of the game. Sean Haslegrave got to the dead-ball line and crossed the ball into Southport's crowded penalty area. Centre-half Chris Dunleavey, under pressure from John Ritchie, appeared to handle the ball inside the box. Referee Hackney, who had a clear view of the offence, immediately awarded a penalty to the visiting side. However, the linesman's flag had been raised and the referee went over to consult him. Much to the chagrin of the travelling Stoke supporters, Mr. Hackney then changed his decision and awarded a free-kick to the home side, claiming that a Stoke player was guilty of 'blatant pushing'. Both sides continued to attack and counter-attack during the last ten minutes of the first half, but to little avail as each defence held steady. Half time;

Southport 1 – 1 Stoke City

As the second half got underway, Stoke stepped up a gear and started to dictate both the tempo and the direction of the match. Under such a continual onslaught, it is of little wonder therefore that cracks in Southport's defence began to appear. Indeed, on the hour, John Ritchie should have scored Stoke's second goal. Feeding off a Jimmy Greenhoff pass, Ritchie sprinted past the Southport 'keeper and fired towards an empty net. Chris Dunleavey, the Southport centre-half responded first and in an amazing turn of speed, Sprinted back to clear off the goal line.

Stoke finally netted what was to be the winning goal in the 70th minute. Following a slow and deliberate build-up, the Potters gained a corner. Sean Haslegrave's Pinpoint pass found John Ritchie at the far post; he hammered it in and **Greenhoff** pounced as Taylor failed to hold onto it, slotting the ball into the back of the net.

Pic. E. Fuller

Greenhoff, now on a high, continued to be a thorn in the side of the 4th division club, having two attempts

on goal in as many minutes. The first was a fierce header from yet another Haslegrave corner, this time thundering against the crossbar. The second, moments later, was a scorching 25-yard shot, forcing Taylor onto his knees as he made the save. Two minutes later Southport were forced into making a substitution as Redrobe, who had run himself into the ground, finally succumbed to a recurring injury and was replaced by Lloyd.

Peter Dobing, despite a heavy challenge, added to the constant assault upon the Seasiders goal with a shot, which flew just over the bar. Southport came back into the game in the last few minutes, as the City players lifted their (collective) foot off the pedal. Substitute Lloyd charged past the Stoke defence and, as John Farmer spread himself in front of the oncoming striker flicked the ball against the bar. Lee then fired a shot on goal which Alan Bloor managed to deflect, despite injuring himself in the process. Within seconds, referee Hackney blew for full-time. Both sides trooped off the pitch to a standing ovation, the gold-shirted home side for their tenacity and the Potters for progressing to the 3rd round of the League Cup for the first time in four years. Final score;

Southport 1 - 2 Stoke City

Adding To Their Education, During A Visit To The City Of 'Dreaming Spires'.

Following their victory at Southport, Stoke were again forced to travel in the 3rd round of the League Cup, being drawn away against Oxford United to play amid the dreaming spires at the Manor Ground on Wednesday 6th October.

The home team, in their yellow shirts and black shorts, included North Staffordshire born – John Evanson in their side. Whilst 'Big' Ron Atkinson missed the game, Evanson, originally from Newcastle-under-Lyme, was lining up against the team he supported as a boy, had attracted the attention of several first division clubs and was being watched that evening by Everton boss Harry Catterick.

Stoke City, in their traditional red and white, made several changes to the side that had faced lowly Southport. Whilst they welcomed back goalkeeper Gordon Banks, they lost the services of defensive stalwart Alan Bloor. Bloor being replaced by Stuart Jump, who played in a sweeper's role, lining up just behind the main defence. Willie Stevenson made a rare Appearance, adding an extra bite to the midfield, when he replaced skipper Peter Dobing. Terry Conroy was back in

Pic E. Fuller

the number seven shirt with John Mahoney reverting to his usual role as substitute. Teams:

Oxford United: - Kearns, Way, Shuker, Roberts, C.Clarke, Evanson, Sloan, Skeen, Clayton, Cassidy, G. Atkinson. substitute, D.Clarke.

Stoke City: - Banks, Marsh, Pejic, Bernard, Smith, Jump, Conroy, Greenhoff, Ritchie, Stevenson, Haslegrave. substitute, Mahoney.

Playing at break-neck speed, both sides set out their stall from the opening exchanges. Oxford nearly

This chapter has been kindly supported by Carl W. Holness.

broke the deadlock in the fifth minute, when, following a quickly taken free-kick, Graham Atkinson's powerful header flew just wide of the upright. John Evanson, living up to his reputation, continued to attack the Stoke goal. Making a run through the centre, he played a one-two with David Sloan before forcing Gordon Banks into making an exceptional save – a move which surely impressed the watching Everton manager.

Stoke broke into the Oxford half in the thirteenth minute, as Conroy brought the ball clear of the City penalty area. Splitting the Oxford defence, his accurate cross-field pass found Ritchie. The big striker, who was showing no signs of his niggling toe injury, ran past Roberts as if he didn't exist. However, the gigantic Oxford 'keeper Mick Kearns spread himself at Ritchie's feet to block the shot. Having claimed the ball, Kearns then made the sort of elementary mistake more often seen on a Sunday league pitch, rather than on the professional stage. Rolling the ball to the edge of his area, he failed to see John Ritchie lurking nearby. The big centre forward nimbly flicked the ball to **Jimmy Greenhoff** who pounced, coolly slotting the ball into the Oxford net.

Once Greenhoff's goal had gone in, Stoke appeared to take control of the

Pic. E. Fuller

game. Oxford attacked, but the defence, led by the resolute performance of stand-in skipper Denis Smith, repelled each foray with ease. Avoiding the two central defenders, Clayton broke free and made a clumsy challenge on the Stoke 'keeper. Banks once again proved why he was the world's number one, by easily catching Sloan's powerful shot, despite the attention of Clayton. Oxford continued to move forward; however, once they got to the last third of the pitch, the City defence closed them down with great effect.

Watched by a crowd of 15,024, Stoke continued to dominate much of the play with their obvious class and determination shining through.

Mike Bernard caused a degree of panic throughout both the Oxford midfield and defence, as in the closing minutes of the half, his bullish run enabled him to get the ball into the penalty area. The resulting shot was unfortunately just wide, smashing into the side netting. Oxford continued with dogged determination, chasing after every ball. Nevertheless, Stoke continued on their relentless march forward. On the stroke of half time, Jimmy Greenhoff slotted the ball forward to Terry Conroy. Conroy's powerful shot was blocked by Clarke – the Oxford man making a desperate last-second lunge to deny 'T.C.' a well-deserved goal. Half-time;

Oxford United 0 - 1 Stoke City

The second half startcd, as the first had ended, with Stoke in the ascendancy. The Oxford 'keeper Kearns, who was clearly upset by the error he made which led to the first goal of the game, nearly repeated it in the opening exchange of the second half. Once again, his lapse of focus nearly allowed Ritchie to steal the ball but he managed to rescue the situation, clearing it into the Stoke half.

By now, City were clearly in control of the game. Stoke, in the form of midfield dynamo, Mike Bernard, once again created problems for the Oxford defence. Racing into space, at a rate of knots that surprised even his own teammates, Bernard met a pass from Sean Haslegrave. However, his lobbed pass was intercepted as none of the Stoke players reacted quickly enough, the ball finally fell kindly enough for Sloan to clear.

Mike Bernard was truly proving to be the thorn in the side of Oxford United, when, following a Jimmy Greenhoff cross, Ritchie headed the ball onto him; his first time volley causing the Oxford 'keeper to make a tremendous save. Always playing with a fluidity, the Stoke attack made an effort to disorientate the Oxford defence by changing their formation, with Terry Conroy switching to the left flank and Jimmy Greenhoff attacking down the right. This ruse failed in its attempt to create further problems for the home - side rather the change worked against Stoke City, themselves.

Oxford capitalised on the disarray during the last 20 minutes of the match, attempting to salvage something from the night. With only twelve minutes remaining, Skeen broke down the right-flank forcing the ball into the Stoke penalty area. In the ensuing melee, stand-in skipper, Denis Smith was knocked to the floor. Despite being pinned down, he still managed to scramble the ball clear. Bouncing free, it came to Newcastle born **Evanson**, whose speculative shot sped through a sea of bodies, unsighting 'keeper Banks, into the Stoke net for the equaliser.

Despite a late flurry by both sides, a replay looked more and more inevitable and so it was to be as referee Walker indicated an end to the proceedings, with the final score remaining;

Oxford United 1 – 1 Stoke City

Graduating With Honours.

It was a sodden Victoria Ground that welcomed both contestants for the 3rd round replay on Monday, 18th October.

In such torrential conditions, both sides changed their line-ups from the first game. The home side welcomed back 'big' Alan Bloor, but not in his usual role, alongside partner Denis Smith, rather adopting a defensive midfield position. Peter Dobing returned in the number ten shirt, with Stuart Jump in for Haslegrave, who was relegated to the substitutes bench.

Oxford manager Gerry Summers brought in Lucas for Way in defence, whilst Trevor Aylott replaced Skeen who was named as substitute. Derek Clarke, the younger brother of the Leeds and England striker Allan, came into the team replacing Cassidy. Teams:

Stoke City: - Banks, Marsh, Pejic, Bernard, Smith, Bloor, Conroy, Greenhoff, Ritchie, Dobing, Jump. substitute, Haslegrave.

Oxford United: - Kearns, Lucas, Shuker, Roberts, C.Clarke, Evanson, Sloan, G.Atkinson, Clayton, D. Clarke, Aylott. substitute, Skeen.

It may be argued that this was the night during which the 'wounded warriors' from the Potteries finally buried the ghosts of the previous season's F.A. Cup semi-final against Arsenal. Gordon Banks' knee was heavily strapped and John Ritchie was still carrying a foot injury, whilst Denis Smith added to the injury woes early in the first half, damaging his knee.

The Oxford defence were soon soaking up the pressure, as wave after wave of attacks from the home side bombarded the visitors penalty area almost from the kick-off. The Potters gained the upper-hand, winning a string of corners, none of which led to a breakthrough, as Kearns made up for his performance in the first game. Having weathered the early storm, Oxford counter-attacked. As the ball crossed into the City penalty area, Gordon Banks leapt, despite a heavy challenge from Atkinson and clung to the ball. The challenge led to a pause in play, as the Oxford player was adjudged to have fouled the Stoke 'keeper. Banks, who despite being hurt in the collision, was able to continue, following several minutes treatment from physio Mike Allen.

During the next twenty minutes, Stoke continued with their assault upon the Oxford goal. Ritchie headed a corner down to Terry Conroy whose

This chapter has been kindly supported by Carl W. Holness.

lightening-fast flick caught the up-right, bouncing out for a goal-kick. 'Big' John Ritchie came close him-self, his strong header being palmed over the bar by Kearns. The big Ox-ford 'goalie' continued to make amends for his errors in the first game, sprinting off his line to deny another powerful Ritchie shot, after Greenhoff had set the Stoke centre-forward free.

The action was almost exclusively taking place in and around the Ox-ford penalty area, as Stoke continued to dominate the replay. Ritchie, at-tacking on the wing, played a deep cross, which Kearns failed to read and the stranded 'keeper must have been very thankful that it was de-fender Colin Clarke's outstretched foot that got to the ball first. Defying the constant bombardment, the visi-tors almost broke the deadlock with a rare foray into the Stoke half. Sloan, breaking down the wing, crossed into the City penalty area, but all his hard work proved fruitless as Atkinson mis-hit his shot, hooking it wide of the upright.

Mike Bernard, collecting the ball in-side his own half from Banks' quickly taken goal-kick, forced his way into the Oxford half with an-other aggressive run. His tenacity brought about yet another corner for the Potters, as the visitors defence was in complete disarray. The result-ing corner led to Stoke breaking the

deadlock in the 30th minute as Terry Conroy's cross created chaos amongst the Oxford defence. The ball finally landed at Ritchie's feet and the big striker shot. Kearns, equal to the attempt, kept it out via his legs, but the rebound went straight back to the big man. Keep-ing his balance as all around lost theirs, **Ritchie**'s second shot de-flected off Roberts into the net, giv-ing Stoke a deserved lead.

Pic E. Fuller

Despite the awful conditions, both sides continued to play an attractive style of football but as the half reached its climax, there were signs that the visitors spirit was beginning to evaporate. As the half-time whis-tle sounded and both sides returned to the shelter of the dressing rooms, the Stoke players had a spring about their step, whilst the Oxford team, to a man, had let their heads drop. Half time;

Stoke City 1 – 0 Oxford United

Oxford started the second-half with renewed vigour, as they pressed toward the Stoke goal. The local lad, John Evanson – formerly of Newcastle-under-Lyme – made their initial foray into the Stoke half, skilfully side-stepping the extended Stoke midfield to take a shot on goal. As in the first game, Evanson was playing under a managerial microscope, this time, Harry Catterick was joined in the Boothen Stand by Bill Shankly alongside representatives of West Brom. Wolves and the Villa.

Much of the Oxford play was now being channelled through Evanson. He was playing in the mould of Stoke's Terry Conroy, utilising both wings as well as the inside channels through which he directed the play. Indeed, the next Oxford attack came, yet again, via Evanson, down the left wing. Skipping over what was fast becoming a bog, he lofted a cross to Clayton. Fortunately for Stoke, the Oxford striker's header lacked power as he attempted to place it beyond the reach of Gordon Banks. Instead, it bounced harmlessly past the 'keepers upright for another Stoke goal-kick.

Stoke, once again, took control of matters as an inch perfect pass by Jimmy Greenhoff found Terry Conroy, sending the flame-haired Dubliner off on one of his famous runs. However, a combination of the condition of the pitch and the presence of fellow Irishman Mike Kearns, prevented him from capitalising on his chance, as the ball was palmed away. Regaining the ball, Conroy managed to slip it to Mike Bernard but the burly midfielder lobbed the ball wide of target.

At that time, both sides brought on their substitutes. Skeen replaced Atkinson, in what appeared to be a tactical move by the visitors, whereas the Potters were forced to introduce Haslegrave into the action, as Jimmy Greenhoff limped out of the game, when he finally succumbed to the groin strain that he had been carrying for some time.

Haslegrave's impact on the game was almost immediate. As the will-o-the-wisp winger overcame the deteriorat-

Pic. E. Fuller

ing conditions, cancelling another assault on the home goal, Mike Pejic galloped down the left-wing and played a long high centre into the Oxford area. Belying the fact that he had been thrown into the cup cauldron only minutes earlier, **Haslegrave** showed an amazing touch as he headed the ball down and hit a crisp volley past the stranded Kearns, putting Stoke 2-0 up.

Down, but not quite out, Oxford valiantly fought on. A David Sloan half-volley brought about the best save of the night, as only minutes from full-time, Banksie once again confirmed his reputation as the worlds greatest goalkeeper by athletically leaping to push the ball over the bar. Haslegrave, once again threatened the Oxford goal when he latched on to Terry Conroy's delicate chip to head just over the bar. Final score;

Stoke City 2 - 0 Oxford United

No Respecters Of Reputation.

The next stage of the 1971-72 League Cup adventure saw Stoke travelling up the M6 to Old Trafford, for the 4th round tie against Manchester United.

The 'Red Devils' were in a state of flux, the heroes of the 1968 European Cup side were disappearing one-by-one and being replaced by players of a lesser quality. Stepney retained his place, despite not being half the player that he once was. Both Dunne and Brennan had gone, being replaced by O'Neil and Francis Burns. David Sadler was the only one of the half back trio still playing – Stiles and Foulkes having been replaced by graduate Alan Gowling, with Steve James playing at centre-half. George Best look-a- like Willie Morgan and Best himself played on the wings. With Charlton, Law and Kidd completing the line-up. Winger John Aston reclaimed the number twelve shirt.

The visitors, Stoke, made one change, with skipper Peter Dobing being replaced by Welsh international John Mahoney. However, the biggest surprise came when the p.a. announcer declared the Stoke number twelve as being George Eastham. Having arrived back in the country 48 hours earlier, following an amazing season in South Africa during which he won the 'Player of the Year' award.

Pic. E. Fuller

He had been given special permission by the Football League to resume his career with Stoke. Teams:

Manchester United: - Stepney, O'Neil, Burns, Gowling, James, Sadler, Morgan, Kidd, Charlton, Law, Best. substitute, Aston.

Stoke City: - Banks, Marsh, Pejic, Bernard, Smith, Bloor, Conroy, Greenhoff, Ritchie, Mahoney, Jump. substitute Eastham.

This chapter has been kindly supported by Carl W. Holness.

13

United dictated the early pace, gaining an immediate advantage by forcing a couple of corners. Bobby Charlton taking them, forced Gordon Banks into punching clear, despite the attentions of Denis Law. Brian Kidd also forced Banks into action as his shot across the goalmouth was finger-tipped wide. Denis Law then broke into the Stoke area, having escaped from his marker Stuart Jump, firing a point-blank shot which Banks smothered.

Tony Waddington, that master tactician, once again shuffled his pack, with Bloor acting as the midfield destroyer. Indeed, this destroyed United's creativity allowing Stoke the chance of getting into the game. Terry Conroy soon capitalised on the extra space, evading the 'Reds' defence to break free but had his shot blocked by Stepney. John Ritchie, in an almost identical move, had his attempt on goal cleared by the outstretched leg of a United defender. John Mahoney continued the onslaught on the United goal, forcing Alex Stepney into making a hasty save. United's defence continued to hold out despite the never-ending bombardment by the Potters. Fullback John Marsh floated a free kick into the penalty area as John Ritchie raced in; unfortunately the big man's header failed to break the deadlock, whistling past the post.

The Potters should have finished the half in the lead following another Ritchie header but referee James disallowed the move, to the amazement of both the City players and their fans alike. It was in the 42nd minute as Jimmy Greenhoff made a Pinpoint cross count, with Ritchie, in the left-hand channel, leaping like a salmon to head the ball past Stepney into the United net. However, the referee adjudged that a Stoke player was in an offside position, thereby disallowing the effort. Half time;

Manchester United 0-0 Stoke City

The second half began as the first had finished, with Stoke piling on the pressure, as wave after wave, they continued to pound the United goal. First came a strike from Jimmy Greenhoff, whose run was capped by a shot that just scraped the crossbar. John Mahoney then went close; blasting the ball goalward, only to see it deflected past the upright. Terry Conroy was the next to threaten the United goal, as the Stoke forwards appeared to be lining up to take turns in attacking the United goal, when his shot just cleared the bar.

United, in what was becoming a rare attack, broke through via Brian Kidd. Kidd's cross was deflected and the United forward's appeal for a penalty was turned down by the referee. Once again, the Potters started to dictate the game as both Mahoney and Ritchie came close to opening the scoring. Mahoney's attempt was beaten out and Ritchie's shot was cleared off the line by David Sadler.

14

The Stoke defence were so dominant that United's forwards became just bit-part players as the drama continued to unfold. Even the magical talents of that flawed genius George Best went largely unnoticed as Bloor continued to stem the flow of decent ball to him. There were, however, moments when he did grace the stage with his undoubted genius. One such occasion, nearly halfway through the second half, saw him holding off a Pejic challenge to shoot at goal. Once again, Stoke's blushes were spared as Banks produced yet another match-winning save, to deny the little Irishman his moment of glory.

The dead-lock was broken in the 72nd minute when Stoke finally got their just rewards. John Mahoney and Terry Conroy combined well in a move down the left-hand side of the pitch. **John Ritchie**

Pic. E. Fuller

ran onto the final pass and, galloping inside, he hammered the ball past the advancing Stepney into the net, giving Stoke that much deserved lead.

With less than 15 minutes to go, United looked down and out, as the Potters continued to dominate the game. The 'Red Devils' were attacking less frequently; however one such attack gained them a free-kick, as John Marsh, misjudging the trajectory of the ball handled it instead of heading clear. Francis Burns, seeing that **Alan Gowling** had been left unmarked, played a cross for the former B.A. student to place a glancing header past an onrushing Banks into the net.

Playing for time, United made a late substitution, introducing winger John Aston into the action as he replaced striker Brian Kidd. In the dying seconds, John Mahoney conceded a free-kick and his forthright protest lead to the Welshman picking up an unnecessary booking. As the referee blew for full-time, the 47,062 crowd gave the visiting side a standing ovation as they left the field. Final score;

Manchester United 1-1 Stoke City

The Epic Adventure Continues.

In what was becoming a regular occurrence during this cup campaign, the Potters faced yet another replay at the Victoria Ground. This time, the 40,829 crowd witnessed the visit of Manchester United.

Once again, Stoke were obliged to change their line-up from the first game. Denis Smith was forced to miss the game due to an ankle injury he sustained during a training session the previous day. With Alan Bloor and Stuart Jump joining forces in the centre of the defence, skipper Peter Dobing returned to take up the captaincy and George Eastham, once again, found himself on the bench.

Manchester United, on the other hand, made only change as Sammy McIlroy, the last 'Busby Babe' came in for Denis Law. Teams:

Stoke City: - Banks, Marsh, Pejic, Bernard, Bloor, Jump, Conroy, Greenhoff, Ritchie, Dobing, Mahoney. substitute, Eastham.

Manchester United: - Stepney, O'Neil, Burns, Gowling, James, Sadler, Morgan, Kidd, Charlton, McIlroy, Best. substitute, Aston.

As in the previous game, Stoke attacked this match with a grim determination and at such a pace as to leave their opponents reeling and rocking on the ropes. Setting about their opponents with a sense of urgency, the Potters defensive tackling smothered the dual threat of Best and Charlton. Indeed, such was the suppression of the two United play-makers, it was of little surprise that the first real chance of the game fell to the Stoke forwards. Terry Conroy freed centre-forward John Ritchie with a pass which allowed the big man the freedom to blast the ball just past the upright. Conroy was proving very difficult to shepherd, as time after time he easily wrong-footed Burns. He and Jimmy Greenhoff combined well during the early stages, pressurising the United defence into conceding a corner. The central pairing of Steve James and David Sadler stood-up to the pressure, repelling the ensuing attack.

Sammy McIlroy made an early attack on the Stoke goal, forcing a corner as the ball shot off Pejic into touch. A solid header from Alan Bloor cleared the danger but the ball fell to the feet of McIlroy, just beyond the penalty area and his 25-yard shot forced Gordon Banks into making an excellent save.

Skipper Peter Dobing, despite a below par performance, created the best chance of the game so far. A

This chapter has been kindly supported by Carl W. Holness.

long-throw specialist, he found Ritchie deep in the United penalty area. The big centre forward flicked the ball on to his striking partner Jimmy Greenhoff, who with his trademark volley, hammered the ball goalwards, his effort failed to break the stalemate though, with the ball rebounding off David Sadler into touch for yet another corner to the Potters. Dobing, himself, went close as Ritchie returned the favour, putting his skipper in the clear. Dobing's blast skimmed the outside of the post, giving United some breathing space. In the dying seconds of the first-half United broke into the City area, through Willie Morgan. The George Best look-a-like connected with a bullet like header to stretch the talents of Gordon Banks - the unflappable 'keeper managing to keep his goal intact by punching clear. Half time;

when manager Frank O'Farrell introduced winger John Aston into the fray.

Jimmy Greenhoff forced Alex Stepney into making a fingertip save, as he capitalised on a combined defensive error from Charlton and Sadler, which allowed him to hammer the loose ball toward the net. The Boothen Enders erupted in the 73rd minute as John Ritchie headed a Mickey Pejic cross into the net. However, referee James, as in the previous game, disallowed the attempt ruling that the Stoke Centre forward was in an offside position. With extra time looming, Welshman John Mahoney ended the half, as the Potters had started it, by attacking the United goal – his long range shot forcing Stepney to push clear once again. Full time;

Stoke City 0-0 Manchester United

Stoke City again put the United defence under pressure directly from the restart with Terry Conroy's extended run gaining the Potters an early corner. United, though made more of their chances in the second half. Brian Kidd, in a fluid movement, split the City defence with a direct run on goal. Stuart Jump was the first defender to react, his speed allowing him to get back to successfully challenge for the ball. On the turn of the hour, Kidd, having failed to make any real impression on the game, was substituted,

Stoke City 0-0 Manchester United

Both teams were evidently tired, but, despite the onset of fatigue, it was the home side that continued to gain the upper-hand, indeed they looked the more likely to score. Eastham, sensing that the United defence wasn't prepared, took a quick free-kick to his midfield partner Peter Dobing. Dobing's probing shot flew just over the crossbar, whilst the second chance, from a Terry Conroy cross failed to make any impression – as John Ritchie who was obviously suffering from fatigue, just missed the ball.

Stoke were left counting the physical cost of a gruelling encounter with both strikers limping through the latter stages of the action – Ritchie with acute cramp and Greenhoff suffering from a recurring stomach muscle injury. Midfield dynamo Mike Bernard also suffered, having damaged his arm in a collision with Bobby Charlton. Full time;

Stoke City 0-0 Manchester United

On an evening fraught with excitement, the Potters did at last come out on top, as the decision for the second replay venue was won on the toss of a coin by manager Tony Waddington. Therefore the 2nd replay was arranged for the following Monday evening at the Victoria Ground.

Pic. E. Fuller

18

What! A Result.

A crowd of 42,233 witnessed this, the, second enthralling replay of a game that went down to the wire.

Yet again, both sides made changes to their line-ups from the previous game. The Potters welcomed back Denis Smith into the centre of their defence for young Stuart Jump, who had been a more than capable stand-in. With manager Tony Waddington once again keeping George Eastham on the bench.

United boss Frank O'Farrell made two changes, as he dropped the less than impressive Brian Kidd and brought in Carlo Sartori. Aston was replaced on the bench by the veteran midfielder Pat Crerand. Teams:

Stoke City: - Banks, Marsh, Pejic, Bernard, Smith, Bloor, Conroy, Greenhoff, Ritchie, Dobing, Mahoney. substitute, Eastham.

Manchester United: - Stepney, O'Neil, Burns, Gowling, James, Sadler, Morgan, McIlroy, Charlton, Sartori, Best. substitute, Crerand.

Unlike the two previous contests, it was the visiting side that made the early running as the special talents of George Best shone through. Best and Sartori linked well as they combined to beat fullback John Marsh. Stoke counter-attacked through Jimmy Greenhoff; his back heel pass just failing to release Mahoney. the first half continued at a frantic pace as both sides continually attacked and counter-attacked. Sammy McIlroy pressed forward and his cross forced a corner, as Alan Bloor calmly headed the ball over his own crossbar. United kept their foot on the pedal through Alan Gowling. His early pass to George Best allowed the talented Irishman the chance to unleash a 25-yard thunderbolt toward the Stoke goal. Banks once again proved his worth; his fingertip save pushing the ball away for a corner.

The deadlock was finally broken in the 37th minute as Alan Gowling, beating the offside trap, found George Best with the ball. Stepping inside, **Best** hammered a right-foot shot across the face of the Stoke goal, past an advancing Banks into the opposite corner of the net. The goal galvanised United into a fresh effort. Best, once again turning on the style, crossing from the left-wing to Sammy McIlroy. The younger Irishman's volley being deflected away for another corner. It was a dejected Stoke side that trooped off the pitch following the half time whistle. Half time;

Stoke City 0-1 Manchester United

This chapter has been kindly supported by Carl W. Holness.

Manager Tony Waddington brought on Eastham for Mahoney during the interval and it was with a revitalised sense of determination that the Stoke players re-entered the seething cauldron of the Victoria Ground. They gained the early initiative by winning a corner. Terry Conroy whipping over a cross, finding John Ritchie hovering above the United defence. His header just failed to make the break through, the ball passing just wide of the upright.

Goalkeeper Alex Stepney was having an inspired night, making three saves in quick succession. Forcing his way though a crowded penalty area, he managed to fist the ball clear despite an onrushing Smith and Ritchie. Defender Alan Bloor created the next chance, thumping the ball forward. Stepney proved equal to the shot as he blocked the ball. It ricocheted to Terry Conroy, who was waiting for the rebound. His first-time shot was also deflected clear by the outstretched legs of Stepney.

Stoke had to soak up the pressure as United once again broke forward. Carlo Sartori broke through the defensive cordon and, as Banks advanced toward him, he side-stepped the diving figure of the City 'keeper – retaining his balance to coolly shoot at the exposed goal. Denis Smith, got back to cover clearing the ball off the line. The ball, rebounded to Sartori whose sec-ond shot on goal was once again blocked by the Stoke centre half.

This was the turning point of the whole match as Conroy broke into the United half with the 'Reds' defender O'Neil bearing down on him. Easily evading the challenge, he ran to the touchline and produced a deep cross to the far post. There was a magical moment in the 70th minute as the flaxen haired Jimmy Greenhoff controlled the speeding ball with ease, laying it off into the path of **Peter Dobing**. The City skipper showed all the signs of his undoubted ability as he equalised.

Pic. E. Fuller

George Best showed his class, and determination, as his mazey run passed three defenders. His shot was less than impressive though as it went wide of the upright. Best was proving to be the proverbial one-man show for United as his next shot hit fullback John Marsh and rebounded out for a corner. Both Bernard and Pejic sustained knocks as they put their bodies on the line but,

20

in reality, it was the United goal that looked under the most pressure with both sides trying to avoid another 30 minutes of extra time. With just three minutes of normal time left Terry Conroy scampered down the wing, crossing to Jimmy Greenhoff. Greenhoff's header forcing Stepney to palm the ball over for yet another corner to the Potters.

The veteran midfielder George Eastham took the kick, floating it toward John Ritchie. **Ritchie**, despite the onset of cramp, soaring like an eagle above the United defence; powering his header into the back of the net. This last gasp goal sealed the victory thereby enabling the Potters to finally progress into the quarter-finals, where they had been drawn to face Bristol Rovers at Eastville. Full time;

Stoke City 2-1 Manchester United

Pic. E. Fuller

Larking About In The Mud.

Following the extended contest in the previous round against the mighty Manchester United, the Potters travelled to Eastville, the West Country home of Bristol Rovers.

In front of a crowd of 33,624 Stoke waded on to a mud patch that just passed as a football pitch, having made just one change to their line-up from the last round. Manager Tony Waddington swapped Eastham for Mahoney, preferring to have the veteran's talents on display from the start. Teams:

Bristol Rovers: - Sheppard, Roberts, Parsons, Godfrey, Taylor, Prince, Stephens, W.Jones, R.Jones, Stubbs, Jarman. substitute, Allan.

Stoke City: - Banks, Marsh, Pejic, Bernard, Smith, Bloor, Conroy, Greenhoff, Ritchie, Dobing, Eastham. substitute, Mahoney.

Rovers, in their blue and white quartered shirts, made the early moves taking the visitors by surprise. The ball fell to Jarman who hammered a shot at the Stoke goal. Fortunately, the City 'keeper was at his best as he tipped the ball over for a corner. He needn't have bothered as referee Nicholson adjudged Stubbs to be offside.

Stoke pushed Bristol back, in the 7th minute, as Alan Bloor brought the ball away from the City penalty area, playing the ball forward to his skipper Peter Dobing who showed a turn of pace that left the Rovers defenders floundering in the mud. His pin-point pass found Terry Conroy coming in from the right-wing, who in turn passed to Jimmy Greenhoff. **Greenhoff,** fending off two defenders, blasted the ball past the despairing Sheppard to open the scoring.

Pic. E. Fuller

This chapter has been kindly supported by Carl W. Holness.

The goal appeared to knock the wind out of the sails of the West Countrymen as they lost their shape. Despite this, Wayne Jones skipped past City defender Alan Bloor to get a shot on target. Once again Banks was alert, tipping the ball away for a corner.

hold on the game as a Terry Conroy shot forced Sheppard into conceding a corner to the Potters. As the penalty area filled with Stoke players, George Eastham played an in-swinging ball into the box. **Denis Smith** rose above both the defence and the 'keeper to head Stoke further ahead.

Pic. E. Fuller

The Rovers corner failed to make any great impression as the rock solid Stoke defence cleared it with ease.

Mike Pejic gave away a free-kick with a foul which warranted a stern talking to by referee Nicholson. The Stoke defenders were caught flat-footed as Rovers took a quick kick. Godfrey's goal-bound shot was saved by Banks who turned the ball away for yet another Bristol corner. Stoke continued to keep a strangle-

By now the visitors were clearly in command and cruising toward a semi-final place but it wasn't all plain sailing. Strongman Denis Smith clashed with Rovers Bobby Jones, a collision, leaving the Stoke man in agony. Later, it was discovered that he had broken yet another bone in his body. Half time;

Bristol Rovers 0-2 Stoke City

Stoke were totally in command as the second half got underway. The difference in skill levels between the two teams was evident as the third division side failed to come to terms with their first division opponents. Greenhoff and Ritchie were running rings around their markers. Indeed, they combined well enough in a move which provided the big man with the opportunity to lash the ball diagonally across the mouth of the goal – flashing past the upright by a matter of inches. Time and time again Ritchie beat Taylor to get a shot on goal but Sheppard continued to deny the big man's efforts.

Both Ritchie and Terry Conroy came close. Ritchie's breathtaking run was ended by the desperate lunge of Prince. While goalkeeper Sheppard denied Conroy, as the Stoke winger broke into Bristol's penalty area, with a last gasp save touching the ball away. Sheppard once again saved the blushes of Rovers, as he made a tremendous point-blank save from the feet of John Ritchie.

However, Stoke put the game beyond both doubt and Bristol after they gained another corner. Eastham's flighted ball found John Ritchie who flicked it on to **Mike Bernard**. His shot, changing directions in the air, left Sheppard rooted to the spot as it flashed past him into the net, making it 3-0 to the visitors.

Pic. E. Fuller

Two minutes later City killed the game as a spectacle by scoring their fourth goal of the night. Greenhoff and Ritchie combined well down the left-flank allowing **Terry Conroy** the freedom to move inside. Receiving the ball and side-stepping the despairing outstretched form of 'keeper Sheppard, to casually flick the ball into the unattended net.

Pic. E. Fuller

Stoke, to their cost, started to coast home having gained such an advantage. This allowed Bristol the opportunity to stage a somewhat belated comeback. Mike Bernard almost gifted the home side a goal, as, in a moment of madness, his powerful back-pass forced Gordon Banks to make a full-length save. Bristol clawed themselves back into the game with just 15 minutes left. Stephens, who was proving to be difficult to contain, was the first to react, when, following a goalmouth scramble, the ball bobbled free. His first time shot was blocked but it rebounded to **Robin Stubbs** who pounced and swept the ball into the net, making the score-line look a little more respectable.

Jimmy Greenhoff, in a moment similar to that of Mike Bernard, played a long back-pass to Gordon Banks, which found Stubbs instead. The Rovers forward failed to advance the home team's goal tally, his tame shot on goal being easily parried by Banks. City nearly scored a fifth goal, as John Ritchie split a totally demoralised Rovers defence with a majestic run that should have ended with a goal but Sheppard once again palmed the ball away. Claiming the rebound the big Stoke striker just missed as his shot hit the side-netting.

The drama wasn't over, as in the last minute of injury time, big Alan Bloor was adjudged to have fouled Stephens, as the Bristolian ended upon the floor. Referee Ricky Nicholson didn't hesitate in awarding a penalty. **Godfrey** stepped up and, giving Banks no chance at all, powered the ball into the roof of the net. Final score;

Bristol Rovers 2-4 Stoke City

The Epic Struggle Begins.

The draw for the 1971-72 League Cup semi-finals brought about an all-London line-up in one tie (Tottenham Hotspur v. Chelsea).

Whilst in the other, it brought together two of the most attractive footballing sides in the 1st division (Stoke City v. West Ham United). While neither were the most 'fashionable' in terms of country-wide appeal, both had the ability and desire to play in an entertaining free-flowing manner. However, both teams added several new dimensions to their character during this epic encounter – which in retrospect was a mini-tournament worthy of the final itself. They both added a grit and determination to the normal talents and emotions that were already evident in their performances. Indeed, these added characteristics created a setting that turned a tie that would usually be played over two legs – home and away – into a titanic struggle which reached its climax after a second replay. There are many who witnessed this tie, either in person or through their television screens who have agreed that it is a match that would have been worthy of the final itself.

The first leg took place at the Victoria Ground on Wednesday 8th De-cember 1971, in front of both a 36,400 crowd and the B.B.C'.s 'Sportsnight' cameras. In fact, David Coleman not only did the match commentary but then he presented the 'Sportnight' programme; live, after the match from the club's own gymnasium.

Stoke City, in their traditional red and white home strip, yet again had to change their line-up from the previous outing at Eastville, as Stuart Jump came in for the injured Denis Smith. West Ham's line-up included Gordon Banks' 1966 World Cup Winning team-mates Bobby Moore and Geoff Hurst and Bermudan international Clyde Best. Teams:

Stoke City: - Banks, Marsh, Pejic, Bernard, Bloor, Jump, Conroy, Greenhoff, Ritchie, Dobing, Eastham. substitute, Mahoney.

West Ham United: - Ferguson, McDowell, Lampard, Bonds, Taylor, Moore, Redknapp, Best, Hurst, Brooking, Robson. substitute, Howe.

Stoke set their attacking stall out from the kick-off with Eastham, in the opening flurry, roaming down the left channel, crossed to John

This chapter has been kindly supported by Carl W. Holness.

Ritchie. The big man's header, much to the relief of Ferguson, flashed just wide of the upright. Alan Bloor also came close, as the Potters built upon the early pressure, his powerful shot forcing the Hammers 'keeper to make a full-length diving save. Bloor kept up the pressure on the Hammers defence up at boiling point, when connecting with another George Eastham corner forcing Bobby Moore to make a hurried clearance from the goal line.

Stoke profited from the fruits of their labours in the 14th minute. Jackie Marsh's adventurous run resulted in a cross to John Ritchie. His well directed header finding Jimmy Greenhoff. Controlling the ball, he fired off a shot that had Ferguson completely beaten. The ball rebounded off the inside of the post to the oncoming **Dobing**. The Stoke skipper side-footing the ball into the back of the net, to give the home side a well-deserved lead.

Pic. E. Fuller

The Potters kept up a constant barrage on the West Ham defence with little more to show for it. In return, the Hammers countered in the form of midfield dynamo Billy Bonds, with Stoke having little idea of how to control this direct threat. The ball was laid out to Brooking on the West Ham left. He sprayed a deep pass into the Stoke penalty area, which led to a certain amount of confusion with Clyde Best ending sprawled out on the floor. Despite the protracted protests from the Stoke City defenders, referee Morrison pointed to the spot, indicating that Alan Bloor was the guilty party.

The atmosphere could have been cut with a knife with England colleagues Gordon Banks and **Geoff Hurst** facing up to each other in a situation reminiscent to the gunfight at the O.K. Corral, with Banks being cast as the 'goodie' and Hurst the 'villain'. The burly West Ham striker running in, his cheeks puffed out, hit the ball with a venomous force. Banks anticipating the direction that his England Team-mate would hit the ball dived to his right. Hurst's kick was too high and accurate for the Stoke goalie, flashing past him into the back of the net for the equaliser.

Despite this setback, Stoke continued to push forward and pressurised both the defence and the goal. Ritchie outjumping Tommy Taylor, his header forcing 'keeper Ferguson into making a great full-length save. Terry Conroy, also proving to be a problem to the Hammers defence, forging past fullback Lampard. Failing to control the winger, Lampard brought him down and was booked for his pains. Half time;

Stoke City 1-1 West Ham United

The Hammers buoyed by their 28th minute equaliser started the second half at a gallop. Hurst gathering the ball at the near post drove a low hard shot on target. The ever-alert Banks, diving full-length, palmed the ball out to Alan Bloor who booted it clear. Mike Bernard was forced to concede a direct free-kick to the Hammers as the visitors continued their advance on the Stoke goal. Young defender John McDowell, eager to get on the score-sheet, smashed his 20-yard effort against the Stoke crossbar. Banks, reacting as the ball rebounded back into play, pushed it over for another corner to West Ham.

As the game was entering the last third, the Londoners appeared to have the upper-hand; beginning to attack – at will. Gaining the ball, Harry Redknapp moving forward, played a diagonal cross-field ball to Hammers striker Clyde Best. Hardly pausing, **Best** collected the low pass at pace and moving into space unleashed a powerful drive, via the underside of the crossbar into the back of the net, thereby regaining the lead for the claret and blues.

Reeling from the setback of West Ham's second goal the home team strove to get back on level terms. Indeed, George Eastham exploiting the space, and made a telling pass into the path of the mobile Jimmy Greenhoff. The darling of the Boothen-Enders sprinted free. Bobby Moore – the England Captain – who had been as imperious as ever in defence, was forced to bring the effervescent Stoke striker down with a professional foul that should have resulted in a sending off. Referee Morrissey however showing a certain amount of leniency by just cautioning the West Ham skipper.

Stoke continuing in their attempt to equalise through a run by Mike Pejic. Attacking down the left wing, he directed a cross toward Ritchie who was advancing into the Hammers penalty area. Ferguson was up to the challenge, punching the ball clear, despite ending up on the floor after colliding with the big striker.

As the minutes ticked away the Potters grew more and more frantic, with each attempt on goal failing to penetrate the last line of defence. Greenhoff, Ritchie and Alan Bloor were all frustrated as the Hammers defence continued to hold out. However, despite the referee's final

whistle the Potters are not down and
out as there is still the second leg
of the game to look forward to.
Final score;

Stoke City 1-2 West Ham United

Pic. E. Fuller

They Paid The Penalty.

It was a rain-soaked Upton Park which played host to, this, the 2nd leg of the League Cup semi-final. West Ham, lining up in their traditional claret and blue remained unchanged from the 1st game at Stoke.

Whilst the visitors – trailing by a single goal - made just one change to the side that was facing their biggest challenge since the previous season's F.A. Cup semi-final against Arsenal. Manager Tony Waddington preferred to play the versatile Eric Skeels instead of Stuart Jump, claiming that the pressure of such a game may be too much for the youngster to handle. Teams:

West Ham United: - Ferguson, McDowell, Lampard, Bonds, Taylor, Moore, Redknapp, Best, Hurst, Brooking, Robson. substitute, Howe.

Stoke City: - Banks, Marsh, Pejic, Bernard, Bloor, Skeels, Conroy, Greenhoff, Ritchie, Dobing, Eastham. substitute, Mahoney.

Tactically, Stoke came out with a more defensive attitude to that of the previous games during the cup run. It was obvious that they were intent on trying to contain the threat of the Hammers attack, whilst hoping to capitalise on any counter-attack.

Bryan Robson, the former Newcastle United forward, was the first to trouble the Stoke defence, his rasping volley flying just over Banks' crossbar. Terry Conroy quickly countered for the Potters, bringing the ball along the wing and crossing it into the West Ham penalty area. Taylor, equal to the cross, headed clear for a corner. Greenhoff posed problems for the West Ham defence, his left-footed shot forcing 'keeper Ferguson to make a diving save as he punched clear. The Hammers, trying extend their slender lead, attacked through Clyde Best. Contacting with the ball, Best's flick beat the outstretched hand of Gordon Banks; however the stoic Alan Bloor tracked back and cleared with ease. As the half came to a close, it was Stoke who were the more dominant, as the midfield trio of Bernard, Dobing and Eastham were coming to the fore. Half time;

West Ham United 0-0 Stoke City

Hurst set the tone for the second half breaking through the City barricades. With the defenders bearing down on him, his shot failing to register, the Stoke 'keeper pounced, taking a clean catch. Countering the Hammers attack, Big John Ritchie broke back and, splitting the defence

This chapter has been kindly supported by Carl W. Holness.

found his striking partner – Jimmy Greenhoff. Spinning, Jimmy Greenhoff instinctively shot toward the near post once again forcing the Hammers 'keeper to fingertip the ball away for a corner. Eastham's corner was cleared as it was just too high for Ritchie to connect with. The Potters continued to pile the pressure on the West Ham goal with Dobing and Eastham teasing and tormenting the Hammers midfield.

In a match full of cut and thrust, attack and counter-attack, West Ham's Best and Brooking combined in a one-two, culminating in Best mishitting the return. Stoke staged an immediate counter, resulting in a freekick to the Potters. Mike Bernard releasing fullback John Marsh with a quick free-kick; desperate to score, the City defender hammered the ball at the West Ham goal. 'Keeper Bobby Ferguson was forced, once again, to demonstrate his agility flinging himself at the ball to deny the Stoke man.

With the last 15 minutes of normal time looming the Potters despite being one goal down on aggregate, were looking the stronger side. George Eastham and skipper Peter Dobing combined well in a movement along the right flank. Eastham's pass gave Dobing the chance to make a telling cross deep toward the far post. McDowell and Taylor

failing to clear allowed the ball to fall kindly to **John Ritchie**. His first time shot flying into the net, with Stoke taking the lead on the night and drawing level on aggregate.

Pic. Courtesy of The Sentinel

As the end of normal time approached and with the thought of extra-time weighing on the minds of both sides, the visitors from the Midlands threw everyone forward in a desperate attempt to break the deadlock. Jimmy Greenhoff causing Taylor to panic with his though ball to Ritchie being intercepted by the centre-half illegally as he handled the ball. This resulted in Taylor being booked. Greenhoff continued to harry the West Ham defence. Terry Conroy breaking free, crossed the ball, for Greenhoff to meet with a diving full-length header. However, this last-gasp attack failed as he missed the ball by inches. Full time;

West Ham United 0-1 Stoke City

The drama didn't finish there as the two teams were level on aggregate - drawing 2-2 - therefore extra time was necessary. The first period of extra time was strength sapping with both sides struggling to overcome the onset of cramp. Despite the fatigue, the tempo remained high – but it was the final touches that began to let the players down. Neither side bothered the scoreboard, with the first period of extra time ending goal-less.

With the second period of extra-time reaching its climax and yet another replay looking inevitable. The true drama of cup football was about to explode, in a 3-minute spell which encapsulated the fears, frustrations and hopes of all involved. Gordon Banks making a rare handling error lost the ball in a goalmouth melee. The ball fell to Harry Redknapp who managed to control it, despite the close attentions of fullback Mike Pejic. Recovering, Banks dived at the ball as Redknapp was lining-up a shot. He got both hands on the ball, but referee Keith Walker judged the City custodian to have fouled the Hammers winger, by being behind him as he dived at the ball. Despite the vocal protestations from the City defenders, the referee pointed to the penalty spot.

Once again, fate had thrown England team-mates Geoff Hurst and Gordon Banks into direct confrontation. This time, however, the hopes and expectations of player and fan alike was much greater as the result of both the tie and the cup run rested on the outcome. It was a moment of epic meaning and proportion as the burly Hurst started his run toward the spot. Several players, from both sides, couldn't watch whilst others bent their heads in silent prayer. As in the first leg, Hurst blasted the ball to the right hand side of Banks' goal. The Stoke 'keeper, anticipating well, dived toward the ball. His dive took him past the ball's trajectory and he had to readjust his angles. Doing so enabled him to palm it over the bar. The save, every bit as impressive as his save against Pele during the 1970 World Cup, in Mexico, was of greater significance – it helped to keep Stoke's hopes alive. Despite this reprieve Stoke still had to defend against a corner. Bryan Robson winning the ball, shot at goal but once again the unflappable Banks connected with the ball, fending it away. As the referee raised his whistle Clyde Best split the central pair of Bloor and Skeels running into a shooting position. His shot, low and hard toward the post was once again stopped majestically by the awesome Gordon Banks. Appropriately the final whistle came as the man of the match - Gordon Banks – kicked the ball clear. Final score;

West Ham United 0-1 Stoke City

38,771 fans witnessed all the emotions that surround a cup tie and would have the opportunity to do so again, as once again a cup tie involving Stoke required a replay to resolve it.

No Winter Wonderland.

A crowd of 46,916 braved the bitter cold and occasional snow flurry to witness the next stage of Stoke's attempt to book a Wembley appearance for the first time in their 108 year history. Both sides arrived at the neutral Hillsboro', the home of Sheffield Wednesday, from their Derbyshire hideaways fully prepared for another epic struggle. The Potters having made just one change to their line-up from the 2nd leg at Upton Park. Denis Smith returned to resume his central defensive partnership with Alan Bloor. Whilst, West Ham, having stayed at Buxton, retained the same team that played in the capital. Teams:

Stoke City: - Banks, Marsh, Pejic, Bernard, Smith, Bloor, Conroy, Greenhoff, Ritchie, Dobing, Eastham. substitute, Mahoney.

West Ham United: - Ferguson, McDowell, Lampard, Bonds, Taylor, Moore, Redknapp, Brooking, Hurst, Best, Robson.
substitute, Howe.

Stoke took the fight to West Ham from the start, with a high cross finding defender Denis Smith, whose header was well saved by the alert Bobby Ferguson. Both Ritchie and Jimmy Greenhoff tried to hammer home the early territorial advantage with shots that were well parried. During these early exchanges, the Hammers were firmly on the back foot, with Stoke continued to threaten their opponents goal. 'Big' John Ritchie was proving to be a real thorn in the side of the Hammers, continuing to run rings around Tommy Taylor. Unlike the previous encounter, the young defender was failing in his attempt to contain the City centre forward. Indeed, it was Ritchie who next threatened the West Ham goal, unleashing a mighty shot which whizzed just wide of the upright.

Skipper Peter Dobing, the club's long throw expert, found the mobile Jimmy Greenhoff with a very accurate throw. His run ended with a shot into the side-netting, much to the dismay of the fans on the opposite side of the pitch. The bombardment on the Hammers goal continued unabated for over 30 minutes as West Ham were kept pinned inside their own half. Indeed, it wasn't until the 34th minute that they made their first serious foray into the Stoke half. Trevor Brooking set Clyde Best free with a square pass, allowing the big Bermudan the chance to burst through the City defence. It became a one-on-one situa-

This chapter has been kindly supported by Carl W. Holness.

tion as he bore down on the Stoke goal. Best unleashed a point-blank shot but Gordon Banks, as ever, proved his worth as he made another instinctive save by pushing the ball away for a corner.

Pic. E. Fuller

The fact that the Hammers goal was still intact despite the constant pressure from Stoke, was down to the form of two men, Bobby Moore and Bobby Ferguson. Moore's class is well documented – but that night he put in a performance which ranked alongside his best. Likewise, the Hammers 'keeper was having the game of his career, taking it all in his stride, even when both he and the ball were bundled into the net by Denis Smith.

The half came to an end as, once again, the Potters threatened the West Ham goal. The ball came to Jimmy Greenhoff, who powered a low hard shot toward the target. Once again Bobby Ferguson was up to the challenge, pushing the ball away for a corner. Half time;

Stoke City 0-0 West Ham United

As in the first half, Stoke started the second period at a gallop. The ball bobbled up in the area during the initial attack and central defender Tommy Taylor appeared to handle inside the penalty area. Stoke players and fans alike screamed for a penalty; an appeal that was roundly turned down by referee Matthewson. In a very uncharacteristic moment the West Ham skipper, Bobby Moore, clattered into Jimmy Greenhoff, thereby leaving the Stoke striker writhing on the floor. The Londoners gained little respite from the constant Stoke pressure as, in a momentary lapse of concentration, Peter Dobing hit a mis-directed pass, gifting a chance to Clyde Best. Best, however, failed to capitalise on his opportunity as the incomparable Gordon Banks quickly reacted and beat him to the ball.

This was the pattern of play for much of the second half with Stoke continuing to dominate the game. John Ritchie, who was playing despite carrying an injury to his left leg, came close as his close-range shot flew inches wide of the upright. Genial Irishman, Terry Conroy also gave the West Ham defence a headache as they they failed to close him down. Having such freedom allowed him the opportunity to sprint through the centre, unleashing a ferocious shot that skimmed just past the Hammers goal. This sparked a further flurry of Stoke attacks, further threatening the Londoners goal as forward and defender alike combined well to pressurise the Hammers defence.

Jimmy Greenhoff forced Ferguson to make a full-length fingertip save as the blond striker's header streaked toward goal. John Ritchie and 'keeper Ferguson clashed as Pejic's long cross flew into the Hammers six-yard box. With the ball bouncing down toward goal, Tommy Taylor, in a covering move, made an awkward clearance. Pejic's co-defender John Marsh also crossed the halfway line to connect with a deep cross from Terry Conroy. The ball flew away, bouncing off West Ham's Frank Lampard for another corner.

Limited, as they were, to the occasional counter-attack, Clyde Best came close as he connected with both the ball and 'keeper Banks, following a cross into the six yard box. Banks once again proved his value to the side, pushing the ball away and then smothering it at the second attempt.

With the conclusion of the second half approaching, the West Ham defence continued to repel the danger of every Stoke attack. Even skipper Peter Dobing came close as two attempts in quick succession were both forced away for corners. Full time;

Stoke City 0-0 West Ham United

The Potters dominated extra time, as they had done in ordinary time. Terry Conroy continued to make inroads into the West Ham half, with each attack forcing the Hammers ever closer to their own goal-line. Dobing reacted to Alan Bloor's pass as he hit the ball on the volley – the ball whizzed just past the post. Once again the physical and mental pressure of the occasion had an effect on the players as Greenhoff was forced to withdraw and even strong-man Billy Bonds gave in to the ravages of Cramp.

Again the drama of the evening did not end as referee Matthewson blew the final whistle on the 0-0 draw. As managers Tony Waddington and Ron Greenwood had to toss a coin to decide the venue of the 2nd replay, Waddo, won, electing to play the game at Old Trafford.

To The Victor Go The Spoils.

For the first time in this extended cup run, manager Tony Waddington, had the luxury of being able to select an unchanged side. His opposite number, however, made one change to his line-up by naming the former Sheffield Wednesday utility player, Peter Eustace on the bench instead of Bobby Howe. 49,247 fans braved this typically cold and wet Manchester evening, to roar on their favourites once more.

This time the majority would not be disappointed as this game, like the others, would be full of incident, excitement and more importantly – a result, which would mean that one team or the other would finally reach the Wembley final, where first division trend-setters Chelsea (who had knocked 'Spurs out of the competition in the other semi-final) awaited them. Teams:

Stoke City: - Banks, Marsh, Pejic, Bernard, Smith, Bloor, Conroy, Greenhoff, Ritchie, Dobing, Eastham. substitute, Mahoney.

West Ham United: - Ferguson, McDowell, Lampard, Bonds, Taylor, Moore, Redknapp, Best, Hurst, Brooking, Robson. substitute, Eustace.

As in the previous match, Stoke took the early initiative, when Jimmy Greenhoff found his striking partner with a backheader. Ritchie's shot was blocked by Ferguson, who, spotting that the big man was unmarked, sprinted out and spread himself at his feet. Billy Bonds broke through the centre to respond for the Hammers but his shot was easily scooped up by Gordon Banks. Once again the game was an end to end affair, with Stoke then West Ham exchanging attempts on goal. Greenhoff had two chances in quick succession; the first forcing Ferguson into making an excellent dive to stop the ball. Next he connected with a John Marsh cross to head the ball just over the bar. A John Ritchie shot also clipped the post after he connected with a pass from Mike Bernard.

There was a moment of controversy in the 15th minute, when the slight figure of Terry Conroy accidentally collided with the Hammers 'keeper Bobby Ferguson as they both went for the ball. It bobbled clear and Jimmy Greenhoff slotted it coolly into the, now, unguarded net. Referee Pat Partridge disallowed the goal, indicating that Conroy had fouled the West Ham United 'keeper. There was a delay, as Bobby Ferguson received treatment.

This chapter has been kindly supported by Carl W. Holness.

He was led from the field in a dazed state, several minutes later as he had failed to respond to treatment from the phsyio. To the surprise of player and fan alike the West Ham 'skipper and inspirational defender Bobby Moore took the green jersey and replaced Ferguson in goal. Speaking after the event Terry Conroy, voiced his astonishment at such a move, by asking why manager Ron Greenwood would allow their most influential player to be placed in a position that was totally alien to him.

Pic. Courtesy of The Sentinel

As is often the case when a team are down to 10 men, they nearly always make more of an effort thereby nulli-

fying the other side's numerical advantage. This was the case on this occasion as, in their hurry to exploit the situation, Stoke lost their shape and composure, as they launched an aerial bombardment on Moore in the West Ham goal.

The stoic Hammers defence finally gave way in the 30th minute as Mike Bernard thundered in to contact with the ball. His strike rebounded off the post back to John McDowell. The young fullback misjudged the sticky playing surface as his backpass to the stand-in 'keeper slowed allowing Big John Ritchie the opportunity to run onto it. Quickly recovering his composure, McDowell chased back, his attempted tackle (from behind) felled the Stoke striker. (John later admitted that for the only time in his career he actually played for the penalty). The referee had no alternative but to award a penalty to the Potters. The drama continued to unfold as the stand-in keeper faced up to the stand-in penalty taker, Mike Bernard. Bernard hit the ball and, guessing correctly, Moore dived to knock the ball out. It rebounded to **Bernard**, who following in, poked it in at the last attempt – scoring for the first ever time with his left-foot. Despite the fact that the ball was nestling in the back of the net, referee Partridge Consulted his linesman before allowing the goal to stand.

Down, but not out, the 10 man Hammers team refused to give in. The balding 'Pop' Robson split the defence, thumping a 30-yard shot on target. Banks was up to the test, making the save look very easy. West Ham equalised through **Billy Bonds**, who ran through two tackles as though the players didn't exist, before hitting a 20-yard scorcher toward the goal. Gordon Banks stood no chance at all with the ball taking a wicked deflection off Denis Smith into the net.

Bobby Ferguson returned to the fray having had a considerable amount of treatment, as the Potters continued to attack. Ritchie immediately put the 'keeper to the test as he had to palm away the big man's header. With the half entering injury time West Ham, now back at full strength, counter-attacked through Billy Bonds. He beat Eastham along the flank, crossing to **Trevor Brooking** whose full blooded volley flashed past Banks to take the lead.

In the last few seconds of the half, Greenhoff started a move down the right wing. He passed the ball on to Eastham who combined well with skipper Peter Dobing. **Dobing,** moving into space, scored with a spectacular shoot that had Ferguson floundering, the ball flying past his outstretched hands into the back of the net. Half time;

Stoke City 2-2 West Ham United

Stoke having gained, both, the lead and psychological advantage when scoring so close to the interval pressed their advantage as they moved forward from the restart. Eastham released fullback John Marsh, who set off at pace along the right flank. His long deep cross was only partially cleared by Tommy Taylor, who contested the ball with Jimmy Greenhoff. The ball fell to **Terry Conroy**. His first time shot screamed into the back of the net past the despairing Bobby Ferguson.

Determined to press home their advantage, Stoke continued to attack at every opportunity. Greenhoff came in for some rough treatment, side-stepping his way into the box before hitting a shot at goal. The Potters were well in command by the 70th minute with Terry Conroy making a clever pass forward to release Peter Dobing. He pushed the ball round the advancing Ferguson but the angle was too acute and his final shot finished up in the side-netting.

West Ham refused to buckle under the pressure as they valiantly attempted a comeback. Geoff Hurst claimed that Alan Bloor had committed a foul in the area but his appeal for a penalty was turned down by the ref. Harry Redknapp also came close as his shot clipped the post before going out for a goal kick. West Ham thought they had equalised after Bryan Robson had netted but he was ruled offside and the 'goal' was dis-allowed. The wait for the final whistle was unbearable as the minutes, then seconds slowly ticked away. Then to a tumultuous cheer referee Pat Partridge finally blew the final whistle – signalling an end to both this epic cup tie and the 108-year wait. The Potters had finally reached a Wembley cup final. Full time;

Stoke City 3-2 West Ham United

We've Won The Cup, We've Won The Cup, Ee-aye-adio, We've Won The Cup.

The final took place on Saturday, March 4th 1972 at Wembley Stadium, in front of a 100,000 crowd on a typically cold, overcast, spring afternoon. The stadium was indeed, both a sight and sound to behold. The tunnel-end was awash in blue and white, whilst the scoreboard-end was ablaze with the red and white of the travelling 'Potters', all waiting for the arrival of their favourite players.

The two teams, Stoke City and Chelsea, led by their respective managers – Tony Waddington and Dave Sexton, emerged from the tunnel, to be met by a cacophony of sound. Following the presentation of the teams to Dr. Gustav Wiederkehr, the President of the U.E.F.A., the two sides split ranks for the pre-match kick-around.

Pic. E. Fuller

This chapter has been kindly supported by Carl W. Holness.

The referee, Norman Burtenshaw, called the two captains together and they - Peter Dobing and Ron Harris - exchanged mementoes and tossed the coin. Dobing won the toss and elected to kick toward the tunnel end, away from the Stoke fans, with Chelsea taking the kick-off.

Pic. E. Fuller

Stoke City, in their traditional red and white striped shirts, white shorts and socks, lined up in a 4–3–3 formation:

Banks,

Marsh, Smith, Bloor, Pejic,

Dobing (c), Bernard, Eastham,

Conroy, Ritchie, Greenhoff.

substitute, Mahoney.

Whilst Chelsea lined up in Royal blue shirts and shorts, with yellow socks, in a 4–4–2 formation:

Bonetti ,

Mulligan, Dempsey, Webb, Harris (c)

Cooke, Hollins, Hudson, Houseman,

Garland, Osgood,

Substitute, Baldwin.

Chelsea set the tone of the game straight from the kick-off. Hollins, who saw that Gordon Banks was off his goal line, received the ball from Alan Hudson and took a speculative but inaccurate shot at the Stoke goal. The early stages of the game were played at a frenetic pace, with Chelsea gaining the early initiative. However, it was Chelsea's Peter Bonetti who was forced into making the first save of the game, as Eastham floated in to the Londoners' half and passed the ball to Dobing, who in turn flicked it toward Terry Conroy, whose 25 yard effort was easily taken.

Houseman failed to keep Dempsey's clearance in play and gifted Stoke a throw-in, just inside their own half. Bernard took a long throw straight to Jimmy Greenhoff, who in turn sprayed the ball to George Eastham on the opposite wing. Eastham's jinking run and cross led to Chelsea's skipper, Ron Harris, clearing the ball for a throw-in just five yards from the corner. Peter Dobing launched a long throw that forced Bonetti into fisting the ball away from his goal line. The ball landed at George Eastham's feet and he floated it back into the goalmouth toward Greenhoff. However, Dempsey managed a half clearance despite the close attentions of both Greenhoff and Denis Smith. The ball ricocheted back off Smith's outstretched boot onto Dempsey's body and flew out toward **Terry Conroy**. The flame-haired striker headed Stoke into the lead from ten yards out, as a stranded Bonetti could only stand and watch the ball enter the net.

From the restart, Chelsea once again set about attacking the Stoke goal. Hollins' long-ball toward Osgood was intercepted by Bernard and then cleared by Eastham to Ritchie on the halfway line. Chelsea hardman, David Webb, then slid through Ritchie in a tackle that knocked the big man off his feet, resulting in a pointless free kick being awarded to the 'Potters'. Hollins cleared the free kick with a long ball forward for Chris Garland to chase. A rather cumbersome tackle by Stoke defender Alan Bloor, saw Garland crash to the ground just inside the

Pic. E. Fuller

penalty area and referee Burtenshaw reaching for his notebook for the first booking of the game. The free kick, about two yards from the penalty area, was taken by Hudson, who rolled the ball inside to John Hollins, the Chelsea deadball expert, who then squandered his chance by firing wide of the upright.

Mike Pejic became the second player to enter Mr. Burtenshaw's book, when, after a Charlie Cooke clearance, he brought Chris Garland crashing to the ground in the twentieth minute. From the clearance of the free kick, skipper Harris lofted the ball back into the penalty area where Gordon Banks made an easy save, his first of the match. Banks' long clearance forced the Chelsea defence into a game of head-tennis, with the ball finally ending at the feet of Greenhoff. His lob forward was knocked back by Webb who forced 'keeper Bonetti into almost conceding a corner.

Hudson and Cooke combined well down the right touchline, but a strong tackle by Bernard stopped the attack when he conceded a throw-in. The Stoke defence continued to hold out despite the pressure from Hollins' long-throw. However, they conceded another free kick as Dobing was adjudged to have fouled Hollins by the touchline. Mike Pejic cleared the free kick with a diving header, giving

away a corner. Houseman's corner pressurised Banks into a rare handling error. Terry Conroy finally scrambled the ball away to Jimmy Greenhoff on the edge of the penalty area. As Greenhoff was sprinting away from the danger area, Peter Osgood cynically hacked him down. This led to a fracas breaking out between Osgood and Conroy, but it was quickly brought under control.

Stoke gained little respite from the free kick, as Chelsea, in the frame of Mulligan, regained the ball and charged down the wing toward the by-line. Pejic, in a well-timed tackle, despatched both the ball and Mulligan over the deadball line. The corner was cleared by Denis Smith, but only to Charlie Cooke, whose right foot thunderbolt from 25 yards out was effortlessly parried down by the world's number one goalkeeper, Gordon Banks. The 'Blues' continued to pressurise the Stoke defence despite being down to ten men, with Mulligan still out of play receiving treatment from the physio Harry Medhurst. From a Hudson throw, Webb once again pumped a highball into the Stoke goalmouth – aimed at Osgood, however it landed at Garland's feet. He turned and blasted the ball toward the right-hand corner of the City goal. Gordon Banks, once again, showed all of his world class, by making a great save, despite seeing the ball very late.

Chelsea's Cooke started a mazy run in his own half, when Hudson, in a tackle that really should have been penalised, stole the ball from Dobing. Easily side-stepping Eastham's tackle, Cooke carried the ball toward the halfway line. Mickey Bernard lunged in and nearly dispossessed him of the ball. Cooke kept his feet and continued his run, with Bernard quickly closing in on him. Bernard's second sliding tackle slowed Cooke down; however he then ran into Stoke's immovable defender, Bloor, whose tackle was deemed illegal by the referee. John Hollins, spotting that the Stoke defence wasn't as organised as it should be, quickly took the kick, floating the ball into the penalty area. Osgood dived and, just beating Denis Smith to the ball, forced Banks to make another good save. Osgood and Smith then squared up to each other, which brought about the third, and Chelsea's first, booking of the match.

Stoke finally succumbed to the Chelsea pressure deep into injury time in the first half, when following Gordon Banks' free kick, Dempsey headed the ball down to Ron Harris. Harris then, in a move reminiscent of Bobby Moore's pass for Geoff Hurst's third goal in the 1966 World Cup Final, booted the ball forward. Smith's diving header cleared the ball for a Chelsea throw, ten yards inside the Stoke half. Harris took the throw to Houseman, who returned the ball to the Chelsea skipper. Harris' forward pass was in-

tercepted by Dobing and cleared by Bloor, but only to the feet of David Webb, just inside the City half. Webb played the ball forward to Garland who, despite the close attention of Bloor, passed it outside to Charlie Cooke. Cooke crossed the ball into the area, hitting **Osgood**, who, despite being on the ground, managed to scramble the ball past Banks' diving frame to provide Chelsea's equaliser.

Stoke, from the restart, moved forward. Hollins dispossessed Dobing, but Greenhoff, in spite of carrying a shoulder injury for much of the half, regained the ball and passed inside to Terry Conroy. Conroy, whose legs seem to extend as he runs, evaded both Hudson and Cooke. Then, side-stepping Webb's despairing lunge, he threaded the ball out to Jimmy Greenhoff on the edge of the penalty area. Getting to the by-line, Greenhoff's cross forced Bonetti into a leaping catch despite Ritchie's presence. He cleared the ball to Cooke who had the last touch of the half as referee Burtenshaw blew to end the half. Half-time;

Stoke City 1–1 Chelsea

Whilst Stoke City remained unchanged at the start of the second half, Chelsea had been forced into

45

making a half-time substitution. Irish-man Paddy Mulligan had failed to re-spond to treatment on his ankle, forc-ing manager Dave Sexton into reshuf-fling his original line-up. Skipper Ron Harris moved to right back, with Peter Houseman slotting into the vacant left back position and substitute Tommy Baldwin replacing Houseman in mid-field.

'Big' John Ritchie set the second half in motion, rolling the ball to Green-hoff, as the 'Potters' now attacked to-ward their fans at the scoreboard-end of the stadium. Greenhoff passed back to John Marsh, whose long forward ball was headed away by Dempsey. Dobing collected the ball and pushed it out to Alan Bloor. Bloor's forward pass through the inside forward chan-nel was cleared by Harris, but only back to Bloor himself. This time he played the ball cross-field to Terry Conroy, on the edge of the penalty area. Jinking inside, he played a diago-nal ball to the feet of the veteran George Eastham. Eastham's attempt to find Ritchie was thwarted once again by Chelsea's Dempsey, whose hurried clearance only got as far as Mike Ber-nard, halfway inside the Chelsea half. Bernard's shot on goal, from some 25 yards, failed to trouble Bonetti as it was hopelessly wide.

Bloor cleared Bonetti's goal kick into touch for a throw-in, despite Osgood's whinging attempt to get a free kick, claiming that Smith had fouled him.

Taking the throw, Harris set the mer-curial Scot Charlie Cooke free. He easily evaded a slipping Eastham as he advanced toward the City half. Side-stepping, he beat both a recover-ing Eastham and Dobing to lay the ball off to John Hollins. Hollins hoisted a high ball toward Tommy Baldwin, only to see Stoke's Denis Smith head clear to John Ritchie. Ritchie sprinted past Dempsey, pass-ing to Greenhoff, whose return, han-dled by David Webb, earned a free kick for the 'Potters'. Alan Bloor, tak-ing the kick from a central position inside the Chelsea half, lobbed the ball to Terry Conroy, who headed it on to Peter Dobing. Dobing flicked it on to John Ritchie who headed the ball past Bonetti into the Chelsea goal. Ritchie however, in evading his marker, had strayed offside and refe-ree Burtenshaw, who was perfectly placed, disallowed it.

Pic. E. Fuller

46

Bonetti's short goal kick found House-man, who threaded a 45-yard inch perfect pass to Osgood, who flicked the ball outside to Hollins. Hollins, with Dobing snapping at his heels, scampered down the left wing and crossed the ball deep into the Stoke penalty area. Bloor, under pressure from Garland, headed it down to Bernard. Bernard, side-stepping Osgood's despairing tackle, brought the ball away from the danger area. He slid the ball crossfield to George Eastham. Eastham crossed the halfway line and passed the ball out to Terry Conroy, who was now on the left wing. Conroy, breaking across field, passed to Dobing who flicked the ball out to an overlapping John Marsh on the right wing. His deep cross caused Bonetti to fumble the ball, taking it at the second attempt. He quickly released the ball to Cooke who dummied Eastham and continued forward. His pass to Hollins, dissecting Eastham and Bernard, found an unmarked Alan Hudson lurking just outside City's penalty area. Hudson passed the ball back to Cooke, who had advanced to a central position just outside the penalty area. In turn, Cooke pushed the ball forward into the path of Baldwin. Baldwin's attempt was foiled by Denis Smith's sliding tackle, which resulted in a corner to Chelsea. Cooke's corner found an unmarked Dempsey level with the penalty spot. His header failed to disturb Banks by flying harmlessly over the crossbar for a goal kick.

Goalkeeper Banks took a short goal kick and the ball was returned to him by defender Mike Pejic. His upfield clearance bounced over Terry Conroy to Ron Harris. Harris, facing his own goal, played the ball backwards across the pitch to David Webb, who then chipped the ball forward to Hudson on the halfway line. Hudson, due initially to the attention of Bernard and then John Ritchie, was forced back toward his own penalty area. Turning the ball outside, Hudson found Houseman on the wing. Houseman's long pass, aimed toward Baldwin, was effortlessly headed clear by Bloor. However, Hollins, in the left wing position, managed to keep the ball in play. Turning, his speculative pass into the centre was easily cut out by Denis Smith. Smith, forced to take the ball toward the touchline, in turn lost it to Chris Garland. Garland's cross was headed clear by Bloor to the feet of Dobing. The Stoke captain sprayed the ball outside to Pejic, whose high ball was misheaded by Webb to Terry Conroy. Conroy's flick was headed on by Greenhoff, but only to Hudson. Hudson's header landed in the path of Webb, whose swashbuckling run continued into the Stoke half. However, his diagonal pass failed to find Baldwin and was easily intercepted by Alan Bloor. Bloor coolly played the ball out to Pejic, who in turn fed it to Mike Bernard. Crossing the halfway line, Bernard passed forward to Greenhoff in the inside right position. He slid the ball back to Marsh who then pushed it forward to Peter Dobing. Turning, he swept it wide to Terry Conroy on the left flank. Conroy dribbled it past Webb to the deadball line and his delicate left-footed cross found Ritchie just beyond the back post. Ritchie nodded the ball down to Jimmy Greenhoff, whose trademark swivelling half volley was palmed away by Bonetti. **George Eastham** pounced upon the loose ball and from three yards out, smashed the ball left-footed past the outstretched arms of Bonetti into the net, to make the score-line 2-1 to Stoke City with just 17 minutes of normal time left.

His long pass was strongly headed away from the Stoke penalty area by Marsh. Hudson, who casually played it outside to Peter Houseman, collected the clearance. Houseman, galloping down the left wing , evaded Mike Bernard's tackle. Bernard recovered and chased Houseman down to complete the job by sliding the ball into touch. Houseman, shaping to take a quick throw, delayed it to allow Hollins to trot across and prepare to launch another long throw into the City goalmouth. The long throw to the front post was fisted clear by Gordon Banks, despite hav-

Pic. E. Fuller

The restart was delayed slightly as Stoke defender John Marsh needed a little attention to what appeared to be a facial injury. However, Baldwin got the game started, sliding the ball to Hudson, who laid it back to John Hollins.

ing to contend with both Bloor and Dempsey's challenge. Bouncing down, the ball reached Terry Conroy whose attempted clearance hit Harris and ricocheted back into the Stoke goalmouth. Dempsey, the first to react, reached the ball, but Gordon Banks spread himself courageously in front of the Irishman's left-footed attempt, causing him to mis-hit the ball across the goal to Cooke hovering on the opposite touchline. Centre forward John Ritchie's covering move forced Cooke into running the ball into touch, conceding the goal kick to Stoke City.

Banks' goal kick found Jimmy Greenhoff, who was evidently struggling with the shoulder injury he had sustained in the first half, following an awful tackle by Osgood. Greenhoff slid the ball to Ritchie deep inside their own half. In turn Ritchie, passed it outside to Pejic. Pejic, surging forward, was harried by Hollins who forced him into touch. Desperate to keep the tempo of the game flowing, Hollins, in his hurry to collect the ball, hit Pejic in the face, an action that really should have resulted in another booking. However, referee Burtenshaw overlooked it and allowed Hollins to take the throw quickly. He threw it to Cooke in the inside right position. Cooke responded by slotting the ball along the Chelsea right for Hollins to run onto. Hollins' attempted cross was resolutely blocked by Alan Bloor, resulting in another Chelsea throw, level with the penalty area. With ten minutes to play, Hollins launched another long throw, deep into the Stoke goalmouth. Webb, getting in front of Bloor, flicked the ball on. Gordon

Banks, once again, managed to clear the danger area, punching the ball away, regardless of Dempsey's challenge. The ball fell to David Webb, whose cross, hitting full-back Mike Pejic, went out for a corner. Cooke's corner met the head of Dempsey, who headed it goal-ward. Alan Bloor, as calm as ever, headed it clear to Dobing at the corner of the penalty area. Dobing's attempted clearance rebounded to himself and he redirected his pass to John Marsh on the other wing. Marsh's forward pass was touched on by Greenhoff to Eastham, who nimbly skipped over Houseman's desperate lunge. Eastham played the ball onto Conroy who channelled it back to George Eastham. Eastham's pass found Greenhoff in the centre, who, despite Hudson's close attention, fed it back to Eastham on the right wing. The move finally broke down as Terry Conroy was adjudged to be offside from Eastham's final pass.

Bonetti's quick free kick was returned to him and he swiftly threw it out to Cooke, just inside the Chelsea half. Cooke, running diagonally across the field, laid the ball off to Alan Hudson. Hudson then pushed it wide to Houseman. Houseman's cross toward Garland was cleared by Bernard, albeit very awkwardly, for yet another throw to Chelsea. Hollins, taking the throw, directed it to Ron Harris, whose cross was deflected off Greenhoff. He laid the ball across the edge of the penalty area to Hudson, whose shot bounced off Cooke. Hudson regained the ball and tapped it out for Houseman to cross it once again. Houseman's cross was acrobatically cleared by Bernard, but only to Cooke. He once again played the ball out to Peter Houseman. Houseman's cross was met by Baldwin, who tamely headed wide.

Stoke, now temporarily down to ten men, as John Marsh tried to replace his contact lens, once again played the ball forward. Gordon Banks' goal kick was headed on by House-man to Chris Garland. Garland flicked it into Alan Hudson who then played it back to his captain, Ron Harris. Harris played it across field to Dempsey, who, in turn, played it forward to Hudson. His floating cross, headed into the area by Garland, was met by David Webb, playing as an out and out striker. Pejic's strong tackle cleared the danger once again, but only for Hollins to spray another pass onto Cooke on the right wing. Cooke again crossed, but this time Bloor effortlessly cleared into touch for yet another Chelsea corner. Cooke's corner was tamely met by Dempsey, who headed on with Gordon Banks taking an easy catch.

Banks' throw was collected by Bernard who waltzed past Garland.

Continuing down the right wing he found Conroy in the inside right position. Conroy passed to Eastham, but the veteran midfielder was hustled off the ball by Ron Harris. Harris played the ball diagonally to Tommy Baldwin. Baldwin flicked on to Alan Hudson, who attempted to play a one-two with Hollins. The return pass, was, however, cut out by Denis Smith. Smith's sliding clearance found touch just inside the Chelsea half. Harris took a quick throw to Charlie Cooke who passed it forward to Baldwin on the right flank. Greenhoff, tackling back, went down on his injured shoulder. Baldwin continued the move, passing inside to Hudson. Hudson could not breach the Stoke defence and the ball once again ended up at Baldwin's feet. His cross was headed clear for a corner by John Marsh. Greenhoff's contribution to the game was over as John Mahoney raced onto the pitch to replace the injured striker.

Peter Osgood met Cooke's deep corner kick at the back post, but his strong downward header was once again saved by an acrobatic Banks. Banks' long up-field clearance was headed out by Dempsey to Mahoney, giving him his first touch of the ball. He played it wide to Conroy, who sprinted to the deadball line. His long cross dissected the Chelsea defence, as well as both

Eastham and Ritchie, to reach Garland in the left back spot. Garland's up-field pass was redirected by Hollins but easily cut out by Denis Smith to Terry Conroy on the wing.

Pic. E. Fuller

Conroy, exploiting the spaces left by a now stretched Chelsea defence, rounded Harris and crossed from the deadball line. Dempsey was forced to concede a corner to the 'Potters'. Conroy's deep corner nearly resulted in Stoke's third goal but Ritchie's powerful header was headed clear by both Houseman and then Webb, but only to Bernard. He lifted it toward

Conroy, but it was cut out by Cooke who fed it out to Hollins. Hollins' forward pass was intercepted by Bernard and hoofed up-field by Bloor. Headed clear, the ball fell to Hudson, whose speculative long ball was headed down by Bloor to Bernard. Mike Bernard, not seeing Chris Garland, made a dreadful back pass to Gordon Banks. Banks, aware of the threat of Garland, spread out and making the save of the game, conceded a corner. Now, in the dying seconds of the game, Hudson took the corner and pumped the ball into a crowded penalty area. Osgood, backing into Banks, gave away a free kick. Gordon Banks' long, high free kick proved to be the last move of the game, when, as the ball reached the halfway line, referee Burtenshaw blew his whistle to bring the game to an end. Final score;

Stoke City 2-1 Chelsea

Pic. E. Fuller

The post match celebrations were amazing. The 108-year wait had finally ended. The scoreboard-end of Wembley stadium was awash with the sight and sound of the jubilant 'Potters'. Borrowing the Anfield theme, they sang "You'll never walk alone" at full volume, whilst the losing finalists were collecting their tankards. Then came the moment that all Stoke fans had been waiting for. Peter Dobing hoisted the League Cup aloft to a tumultuous cheer. He was followed by John Ritchie, Alan Bloor, Denis Smith, the injured Jimmy Greenhoff, Mike Bernard, the scorer of the winning goal - George Eastham, Mike Pejic, Gordon Banks, substitute John Mahoney and, finally, the scorer of the first goal - Terry Conroy. Everyone a hero!

The band played the national anthem but not one Stoke fan heard it; they were all singing, "We've won the Cup". Then came the lap of honour. The Chelsea players chose to walk straight back to their dressing room, whilst the Stoke fans went delirious. Then came a sight that showed the real bond between the boys of '72 and their faithful supporters, when those heroic players returned their adoring fans applause.

Pic F Fuller

Pic. E. Fuller

53

Pic. E. Fuller

Pic. E. Fuller

Pic. E. Fuller

Pic. E. Fuller

The Players

1

Pic. E. Fuller

Gordon Banks O.B.E.

Born 30th December 1937 in Sheffield, 'Banksie' joined Stoke City in 1967 for £52,000 from Leicester City. A member of the victorious 1966 World Cup winning side, he played in 11 of the 12 games in the League Cup run.

This chapter has been kindly supported on behalf of Sue Boughey.

Born in Sheffield on 30th December 1937, Gordon was the youngest of four brothers. His prowess between the 'sticks' soon brought him to the attention of the Sheffield Schools selectors. However, unlike many of the boys who represent their own district/town/city/county side, this wasn't a direct stepping stone into the world of professional football for the young Yorkshire man. Indeed, his next game between the posts came courtesy of the local team, Millspaugh - who's regular 'keeper had failed to turn up, so Gordon was asked to deputise.

Pic. Eddie Fuller

Combining his life as an apprentice bricklayer with his weekend alter ego as a goalie, Gordon soon came to the attention of Chesterfield, who duly signed him as an amateur. He quickly made an impression with the Derbyshire club and was taken on as a semi-professional – for the princely wage of £2 per week. Still an amateur, he played for the youth and reserve sides with the Spire-ites – indeed he played an important part in their youth-team's progression to the F.A. Youth Cup Final in 1956, where they unfortunately lost 4-3 to Manchester United at Old Trafford.

A full time career beckoned, but his progression into the professional ranks was interrupted by the call up to do his national service. Following two years in Germany, where he met and married Ursula, Gordon returned home to be greeted with a professional contract from the Saltergate club. An instant success, he quickly claimed the 'keepers shirt as his own and with it came overtures from larger clubs. Indeed, after only 23 1st team games, Chesterfield accepted an offer of £7,000 from Leicester City's Matt Gillies for him. So the talented young 'keeper made the southerly move to Filbert Street in 1959.

Despite fierce opposition from five other 'keepers, Banksie quickly established himself as Leicester's number one choice. Two seasons after his 1st team debut he made the first of many appearances at Wembley Stadium as the Midland side got to the F.A.Cup final where they met Tottenham Hotspur. 'Spurs who had swept all before them in the league, became the first team in the century to complete the double as they won 2-0.

During the 1962-63 season, Gordon returned to the hallowed Wembley turf on no less than three occasions. Unfortunately finishing on the losing side twice, as firstly he made his international debut against the 'Auld Enemy' and then in his second F.A. Cup final appearance against Manchester United, before being in the England side that drew 1-1 with the mighty Brazil.

The following season, '63-64, saw Gordon and his Leicester City team-mates win their first domestic honour when they won the then two-legged League Cup final 4-3, paradoxically against Stoke City. Indeed, as Peter Dobing recalls of his future team-mate; "Banksie won the cup for them with his performance in the 2nd leg alone, as despite our domination, he continued to repel every shot".

By 1966, Banksie was an England regular, despite the muted comment Alf Ramsey made to Gordon after one international; when, as they were leaving the team hotel, Gordon bade his manager farewell, saying "I'll be seeing you Alf". To which the England boss replied, "will you?" This retort was intended to keep the goalie on his toes and it worked, as he was an ever-present during the 1966 World Cup winning campaign.

England, the host nation, kicked the 1966 tournament off with a less than inspiring goalless draw against Uruguay. Five days later, their campaign received a jump-start as they beat Mexico 2-0. The final group match saw the host nation beating France 2-0. Having qualified for the quarterfinals they met Argentina in a match that will forever be remembered in the annals of history because of the appalling behaviour of the South American players. Indeed, Alf Ramsey later described the Argentinians as nothing more than "animals". A single goal decided the tie as Geoff Hurst secured the host nation a semi-final slot against Portugal.

Gordon was obviously proud of getting to this stage of the competition without conceding a single goal. However, Jack Charlton was forced to handle the ball in the area during the semi-final against Portugal, giving away a penalty. Eusabio duly

despatched the ball past Banks, but as Bobby Charlton replied by scoring twice, England won through to the final – where they would meet West Germany.

30th July 1966 is the day that is engraved upon English footballing history as Alf Ramsey's eleven heroes; Gordon Banks, George Cohen, Ray Wilson, Nobby Stiles,

Jackie Charlton, Bobby Moore, Alan Ball, Roger Hunt, Bobby Charlton, Geoff Hurst and Martin Peters soundly beat the West Germans 4-2 in a thrilling match, to become World Champions.

Returning to the normality of club football, Gordon was more than a little surprised to find himself surplus to the needs of Matt Gillies' Leicester City, who announced that they would be open to offers for the great man, as they had a ready made replacement in the shape of (a certain) Peter Shilton already chomping at the bit. Desperate to prove to both Gillies and Leicester that he wasn't ready for the scrapheap at 29 years of age, he joined Stoke City in March 1967, for a fee of £52,000.

An instant hit with the Victoria Ground faithful, Gordon's career went from strength to strength, both on the club and international stage as, by 1970, he was considered to be the greatest 'keeper of all time. He didn't do anything to harm this opinion of himself, rather he enhanced his status, especially by making what has become known as the 'save of the century' during the group match against Brazil, which is still occasionally seen on television today. It was the end result of a move started by the Brazilian skipper Carlos Alberto. His amazing pass curved past the England full-back Terry Cooper – straight to the feet of the accelerating Jairzinho. The speedy, diminutive, winger sailed blithely on leaving Cooper standing. As he raced to the by-line, Tostao made a darting run toward the front post. Gordon moved across to cover this situation; however the flying winger's cross was much deeper, intended for Pele, who arrived like an exocet missile to head the ball goal-ward. Somehow, Gordon prevented the ball from entering the net, as in one movement, he turned, sprinted across the goal line and, diving, he managed to tip the ball over for a corner. This amazing save didn't satisfy Gordon, as Jairzinho later scored what turned out to be the winner. England, minus Gordon, went out at the quarter-final stage, losing 3-2 to West Germany.

Returning home as the world's greatest goalkeeper, Gordon continued to perform at the highest standard for both club and country. Indeed, he was more than instrumental in the Potters successes in the 1970-71 F.A.Cup run. He was the pivotal player during the passage of play that led to Arsenal's equaliser in the 1st semi-final at Hillsborough. Nobody can deny that he was fouled, but the ref. didn't see it at the time and awarded a free kick to the Gunners. They won a penalty as Josh Mahoney punched the ball clear. He stood no chance as Storey coolly slotted it past him, earning the lucky Londoners a replay. Once again,

Arsenal rode their luck and won the following Wednesday evening's replay.

The following season saw Stoke mount a double assault on the major domestic trophies – the F.A. Cup and the League Cup. Gordon missed the first match of the League Cup run at Southport

Pic. E. Fuller

as he was suffering from a bout of 'flu. Despite John Farmer proving to be a more than adequate deputy, Banksie returned for the Oxford match and retained his place for the rest of the run. He came to the fore during the epic semi-final clashes with West Ham United. In the 1st leg he was soundly beaten by a Geoff Hurst penalty, then in the 2nd leg, after a mix-up with Mike Pejic, Gordon was adjudged to have brought down Harry Redknapp. Once again it was like a scene from 'Gunfight at the O.K. Corral', as in the dying seconds of the tie, England colleagues Geoff Hurst and Gordon Banks squared up to each other. The burly forward blasted the ball toward the net, in exactly the same manner as he had done in the previous encounter. Banksie guessed where the ball was going and dived. He had to slightly re-adjust his movement, but still managed to parry the ball away, thus earning Stoke another bite of the cherry. He played his part in the game at Hillsborough, when, following a momentary lapse of concentration from Peter Dobing he was called into action to prevent Clyde Best from scoring. Following that came the glorious night at Old Trafford, as the Potters fought through to their first and Gordon's third Wembley cup final appearance.

He walked onto the Wembley turf for a third time in a club match, determined to make up for the two previous defeats he had been part of. He denied Osgood and Garland in the early exchanges from making an impression upon the score-line. Whilst at the other end of the pitch, T.C. headed the Potters into the lead within the first five minutes. Chelsea's equaliser was the result of a scrappy interchange, which led to Osgood sliding the ball past Banks. He was called on to make several saves throughout the game, however, all of his strengths as a 'keeper were called into action when a Mike Bernard back-pass caused great concern, as the ball by-passed both Smithy and Bluto, with Garland sprinting toward it. Banksie, aware as ever, sped out of the box spreading himself in front of the oncoming Chelsea man, he pushed the ball away for a corner. A few minutes later, the final whistle ended the game and Gordon had finally broken his hoodoo - winning a club trophy at last! A second F.A. Cup semi-final approached with the promise of another Wembley appearance as the prize. Stoke were once again beaten by Arsenal and some dubious refereeing decisions. However, Gordon did finish the season on a high as he won the Footballer of the Year award.

The '72-73 season kicked off with Banksie once again in an upbeat mood, as he continued to put in an amazing performance week after week, in both the league and U.E.F.A Cup with Stoke and for England as they prepared for the 1974 World Cup Finals. Then came the weekend in October which changed his life forever.

Stoke travelled up to Anfield on Saturday 21st October to play in what proved to be Gordon's last ever league match. The Potters took the lead and were looking as though they would earn a rare victory on Merseyside. Then, within a 15 minute spell, the Kopites were in full vocal refrain as they took the lead back. Gordon's final action of the day occurred after the referee's final whistle. His over-enthusiastic remonstrations with Roger Kirkpatrick led to a booking. The following day, after a visit to the ground for some treatment to a slight injury, he was involved in a serious car accident which cost him the sight in his right eye. So, after a distinguished career which had included 73 England caps, it appeared that his playing days were over.

Stoke City stood by Gordon and he became the youth team coach. However, he was given the chance to resurrect his playing career in the United States, with the Fort Lauderdale Strikers in the North American Soccer League. Following a two year stay in the States, during which time he won the League's Goalkeeper of the Season award, he returned to his native shores and despite his reputation as the world's greatest keeper Banksie only received two job offers. He chose to stay in North Staffordshire and joined the backroom staff at Port Vale. Following that, he had a time as manager of non-league Telford United.

Having departed from the Vale, Gordon ran his own sports and country club on the outskirts of Stoke-on-Trent. He later moved into the sports promotion business in Leicestershire, before moving back to North Staffordshire, where he lives today. He is still involved in the world of football, alongside his former international team-mate Roger Hunt, as a member of the football pools panel, which meet every week. Further to this, he is also a part of the Stoke City scene again, when following the death of Sir Stanley Matthews, he became the club's president.

Looking back at a tremendous career between the 'sticks' we can surely say that Stoke and England's goal, under the stewardship of Gordon, was 'as safe as the Banks of England'.

2

Pic. E Fuller

John Marsh

Born on May 31st 1948, in Stoke-on-Trent. Jackie joined Stoke City in 1963. Rising through the ranks, he made his 1st team debut in August 1967 at Highbury. Jackie was an 'ever-present' during the League Cup run. A strong defender, he was also renowned as an excellent attacking full-back whose forays along the wing caused problems for many an opponent.

This chapter has been kindly supported by Roger Martin.

Fenton born, John was a product of the successful City of Stoke-on-Trent Schools side, which retained the English Schools Shield in 1962. Who progressed to the professional ranks at the Victoria Ground and by doing so. He realised an ambition he had held since he was eight years old. Looking back, John recalls both his early ambitions and the shield run that led to his contract, saying: "I always supported Stoke; as a boy I lived about a mile away from the Victoria Ground and would go via a place called 'Carters Crossing' to see the heroes of my day (whilst standing on the Boothen End). Players such as Bill Robertson, Ken Thompson, Tim Coleman and Johnny King were all regulars and as a kid, I would go home and join in a kick around in the street pretending that I was Johnny King. Then, I played for Queens Street School in Fenton and was good enough to get into the City of Stoke Schools team in the 1961-62 season, alongside boys such as Bill Bentley, Denis Smith and John Woodward (all of whom went on to join Stoke) and Clinton Boulton (who joined the Vale), under the watchful eyes of Dennis Wilshaw and Cecil Finney. We went on to win the Shield, but not until we had played in the most amazing game that I have ever been involved in. We played Wrexham Schools in the 1st round at the Racecourse Ground and with 15 minutes left were losing 5-1. Dennis brought on Graham Bird (from Blurton High School), who quickly scored a hat-trick and with just a couple of minutes left, we were leading 6-5, then they won a corner. Mickey Starkey, our centre forward came back to help in defence and promptly scored an own goal making it 6 all. So, we had to have a replay at Northwood Stadium, which we won 5-0. The rest is history as we won our way through to win the competition beating Tottenham in the semi-finals before defeating Bristol in the final itself. Several of that team went on to join Stoke at the end of the competition, including me. So, in 1963 I became an apprentice professional at the Victoria Ground".

It was the right time to join the Potters for John, as he was able to witness the promotion season at first hand. What does he recall of that era? "I remember that I was on £7.00 a week, but wouldn't have changed a thing. To actually be a part of the club that I had supported ever since I was an eight year old was, in reality, a dream which came true. It was an amazing time, being in the dressing room when we had such great players as Eddie Stuart, Eddie Clamp, Jimmy O'Neill and of course, Stanley Matthews. I'll never forget Stan scoring the goal against Luton Town which secured promotion for us. It was just a fantastic feeling to have been a tiny part of that moment, even though it was only a small part behind the scenes. Not only was there an array of talent and experience in the side, but there was an abundance of character as well. I remember that my pay was boosted by the princely sum of a pound each week by Eddie Clamp, for polishing his boots and 'looking' after his studs" (laughs).

John progressed through the ranks and finally made his 1st team debut in 1967, when the Potters travelled to meet Arsenal at Highbury. However, when looking back at those early days, he not only remembers his debut, but of playing in the same reserve side as the legendary Stanley Matthews, when he says: "I was lucky to play in the same side as Stan, when he was returning from injury and having a run out in the reserves. Although I couldn't really go on any of my over-lapping runs because I wouldn't expect him to challenge back for me. Then, in 1967, Tony gave me my chance at Highbury. In those days the team list didn't have to be handed in until the last minute so I didn't know I was making my debut, by replacing the injured Eric Skeels, until about 20 minutes before the match itself. On the plus side though, neither did the Gunners, so they

Pic. E. Fuller

couldn't really exploit my inexperience could they? (laughing) I also seem to remember that it was Peter Hewitt's first match report for the Evening Sentinel and obviously nobody had bothered to tell him of the change to the side, as the column kept saying: 'Skeels beat Armstrong to the ball' and 'Armstrong got the better of Skeels during the latter stages' etc. It wasn't until you read the stop press where it said 'Marsh replaced Skeels in the starting line-up' that he noted that I was playing".

John felt that Waddo didn't pressurise him by playing him week after week, rather he brought him on gradually. However, by the semi-final years, '70-71 and '71-72, the back four basically chose itself. The side had been rebuilt and at its foundation was the home grown defensive unit of Marsh, Bloor, Smith and Pejic, so it must have been a great shock to John when Waddo announced the line-up at Hillsboro' to find that he wasn't being included. "It was one of the most disappointing times of my life, as I'd played in every game during the cup run and, with just 20 minutes to kick-off, Tony announced that Eric would be playing instead of me. What disappointed me more than being replaced, was the fact that Waddo never explained his reasons to me. We all know the result, but what really struck me was the atmosphere on the coach as we returned home from Sheffield. We all felt deflated and weren't able to pick ourselves up for the replay".

The following season saw the Potters make another concerted challenge for the major domestic honours. An effort which resulted in the ending of a 108 year wait as they finally reached the League Cup Final at Wembley. John certainly played his part in that cup run, taking part in all twelve games. In hindsight, what does he recall of that momentous season and of the cup run itself? "The first game was like a banana skin waiting for us to slip on it; fortunately, we didn't, as Bluto set us up for a victory with a well-taken goal. At that stage of a competition, you just want to progress to the next stage and we did just that, beating Oxford after a replay. I recall that we had hoped for a 'plum' draw in the next round and that's just what we got against Manchester United. Not only did we get a choice tie, but we also started thinking about the possibility of winning the cup itself. George's return from South Africa boosted the feeling within the squad and I'm sure that we deserved the overall victory, even though it did take

us the three games to achieve it. The quarter-final was less of a challenge as we won easily and then onto the epic struggle in the semi-finals against West Ham United. Like us, they were another side who played entertaining football. I don't think that playing at home did us any favours and with Denis missing it, made it a little harder. Going down to Upton Park one goal down was going to prove difficult, but 'Big' John put us right back into the game with his great goal. Then came Banksie's save, which I think was the moment which finally swung the momentum in our favour. I remember the journey home after that game and couldn't help comparing the atmosphere between that and the trip home from the previous season's F.A. Cup semi-final. This time there was an air of self-belief amongst us and I'm sure that was what finally got us into the final after the two replays".

Jackie Trent and Tony Hatch
Pic. E Fuller

Then the build up to the final itself began in earnest and the (now inevitable) record was made. Which, as John recalls, didn't exactly go to plan for two of the players who were at the recording session: "We were in the studio and after a second rehearsal, Tony (Hatch) entered the room and as we ran through the song for a third time, he indicated to Terry Lees and myself to stop singing. He then explained that our voices were much to deep and asked us just to mime. Neither of us wanted to do this, so we went into the sound engineer's booth and had several cups of tea, whilst the others continued to sing".

Onto the final itself, after a week away in London, as John says: "You can't put into words what it meant to us as we walked out onto that pitch. It was the proverbial dream that came true – especially for those of us who were local lads and had supported the club as youngsters. Looking back at the day itself, I think there was an undoubted difference in the attitude or body language between the two sides as we lined up to walk onto the pitch. We were buoyant – it was our first visit (as a team) to Wembley and we went out to enjoy ourselves. Whereas Chelsea looked as though they had all the troubles in the world upon their shoulders. After all, they had been knocked out of both the F.A. Cup and the European Cup-Winners Cup in the week before our final. So I feel that this did indeed add an extra pressure upon them. Really they should have risen above this pressure, but they didn't cope as well as we did on the day. Whilst we didn't have any specific instructions to play a more defensive role than usual, both Pej. and I recognised the dual threat of Cooke and Houseman. So we deliberately kept our overlapping runs to a minimum. Early in the game, I got a knock in the face, which looked far worse than it actually was. Then came the period in the second half, which everybody always brings up in conversation with me, when I lost my contact lens. Chris Garland and I challenged for a loose high ball and his elbow caught me in the face and dislodged my contact lens, just as the ball went out for a Chelsea corner. As we lined up in the box, I told Smithy about my problem, which in hindsight, (no pun intended) wasn't the best moment to tell him that I couldn't see properly. However, we cleared the ball and then I was able to restore my vision, with a little help from Mike Allen our physio."

As the full time whistle sounded, the players celebrated a tremendous victory, but what did it really mean to John, as one of the local lads? "I must admit to a few tears as I looked up at the scoreboard which read Chelsea 1 Stoke City 2. It was also such a joyous occasion, especially as we could celebrate it with all our loyal fans. To be a part of that day was just so special and we could feel the warmth of emotion from our supporters as we did our lap of honour. It is something that I will never, ever forget. The celebrations continued through the night, but the following day was something very special indeed. We arrived back at Barlaston and travelled through the Meir, then Longton and Fenton on our way to the civic reception at the Kings Hall in Stoke. As we went through Fenton, I saw so many friends and people that I knew, who had come out to welcome us home; it was just so unbelievable and in retrospect, was probably emotionally more important (to me) than the match itself".

John's career with Stoke continued until the 1978-79 season. However, during 1976, he had a break as Waddo allowed him to join the Los Angeles Aztecs on loan. He played alongside the likes of George Best, Charlie Cooke and Ron Davies, admitting that it was a wonderful experience. He also recalls that: "Tony Waddington contacted me during my stay in America, asking me for Georgie

Best's 'phone number. A few days later Bestie came over to me during a training session and said: 'I've had a call from your Gaffer asking me if I'd like to join Stoke when we get back to England'. Unfortunately George went back to Fulham instead".

By '77, Waddo had been replaced by Alan Durban, who was attempting to stamp his authority on the club by rebuilding the side. This meant the departure of many of the older players, such as Bluto and Jackie, who remembers that: "To be fair, I didn't see eye to eye with Durban's philosophies, but I wouldn't decry what he did for the club, so I left for pastures new, joining Paul Ogden at Northwich Victoria. It wasn't just a culture shock but also a feeling of great disappointment for me, as I realised that my days with the club that I had supported as a boy were finally over".

This was followed by a stint in Hong Kong with a side called Kuitan, which he says was, "like playing amateur football but the experience that I had whilst living in the country was fascinating". He returned to Stoke-on-Trent in 1980 and has stayed in the area ever since. Today, John is still very interested in his own team's affairs and can be seen at the Britannia Stadium at most home games, as he casts his critical eye over the players of today.

Pic. E Fuller

3

Pic. E Fuller

Mike Pejic

Born in Chesterton on January 25th 1950, 'Pej' was also an ever-present member of the League Cup winning side of 1972. Like Jackie Marsh, Pej came through the ranks having joined Stoke in 1964. He made his 1st team debut in 1968 against West Ham United.

This chapter has been kindly supported by Andrew Hine.

Mike Pejic's love affair with Stoke City began when he was just 5 years old. He was taken to watch Stoke play by his father and grandfather. He well remembers sitting astride the crush-barriers on the Boothen End, watching his new found heroes and dreaming, as all youngsters do, of one day donning the famous red and white jersey and playing for Stoke himself. Unlike the ambition of the many, his dream was to come true, as he became a 1st team regular in 1968.

Born in Chesterton in 1950, Mike started playing football as a child. He soon came to the fore, initially playing for his school and then for Newcastle-under-Lyme schoolboys. He soon became a regular performer for the district side and continued to do so, until his fourth year at senior school. Following a disagreement with his teacher (who was also on the district selection committee), he was not chosen again. However, as one door closes another is sure to open and this proved to be so for the young fullback.

One evening, in 1964, Mike's father took him down to a training session run by Frank Mountford, the clubs 1st team trainer at Stoke's Victoria Ground, for promising youngsters. Following the introductions, Mike was allowed to train alongside players who were four or five years older than himself; players who were regulars in the 'B' team. It was, as Mike recalls: "a very gruelling time, but it was very beneficial to me and the club, as they offered me terms in 1967. I remember that we would finish each session with a five-a-side game below the Boothen End, with the toilets at each end being used as the goals and the walls and steps being the touch-lines".

The next season saw Pej playing three games each weekend, including regular appearances for Kingsley juniors, (which was the then Stoke 'B' team) in the Leek and Moorland league. Twelve months later, he was invited to take part in a large-scale trial match, which involved about 90 lads. "I was one of just three lads who were signed up. In my case, it was on a twelve-month apprenticeship. Then on my 18th birthday (in 1968), I signed a full professional contract".

Pej soon laid claim to the number three shirt and, by his next birthday, was considered a regular 1st team player, but what does he remember of his 1st team debut against West Ham United? "Quite a lot really, because I had no indication prior to that morning that I was even in the squad. It was about 11.30 in the morning, when Tony came up to me and told me that I was in the squad to travel down to London for that nights game against the 'Hammers'. I had to dash home and get my things and rush back to the station, getting there just a couple of minutes before the train left. We travelled down to London and booked into the hotel. I still didn't know that I would be playing. We arrived at Upton Park about an hour before the game and it was then that Waddo told me I was playing. Looking back, it was probably the best way of telling me, as I didn't have any time to worry about the game itself. I marked the 'Roadrunner' as we called Harry Redknapp. It was quite an interesting game as we came away with a well-earned draw, as I remember".

Having played well on his debut, the young defender probably expected to retain his place for the next match, which was also in the capital, this time against Q.P.R. But this was not to be the case. Why then, didn't Waddo select him after making such an impressive start? Many observers have suggested that Waddo chose to do this to keep the young Pejic's feet firmly on the ground and also to make him hungrier for success. It was surely a ploy that worked, as Mike is still as friendly and level-headed today as he always has been, and it did indeed make him fight to reclaim the number 3 shirt. Indeed, as Mike recalls: "The same thing had occurred when I made both my reserve and home 1st team debut against Sunderland; however it did make me more determined to make that number 3 shirt my own in time".

At this time Pej, like Bernie and Smithy, was determined to put something back into the game and did so by coaching a local Sunday league side. Mike remembers that: "All three of us were so competitive and when our paths crossed on a Sunday morning, the games took on an extra meaning".

By 1970, Waddo had put the finishing touches to his side and, apart from injury, drop in form, or suspension, the team really picked itself. This, obviously, led to each player having a greater understanding of how the rest of the team would react. Indeed, this especially applied to the defensive unit of Jackie, Bluto, Smithy and Pej, who playing in front of the world's greatest goalkeeper, were proving difficult, to say the least, to penetrate. Added to this experience was the feeling in the back row, as Mike recollects: "Not only did we work well as a unit, but we also had confidence in each other. Further to this, we felt invincible as we had Gordon behind us. There was also a special bond between the four of us. We were all local lads and had strong feelings for the club. I think the fans related to this as we had a special relationship with them and this made the four of us even more determined to do our best for the club". This proved to be the case as the Potters progressed to the semi-final of the F.A.Cup, where they were to meet the 'mighty' Arsenal. Mike recollects that: "We went 2-0 up and played extremely well and really should have had it all wrapped up, but we let in two goals in a rather extended second half, which was a serious blow to us". He continued by saying; "I think it was our best chance because we didn't manage to get into our stride at all during the replay. Looking back, I think that I was lucky to have stayed on the pitch as I'd been involved in an incident with John Radford, for which, in all honesty, I think I should have been sent off. However, Pat Partridge showed a certain amount of understanding and leniency as he just lectured me instead. From that moment on, he gained my respect". A respect which is still evident today, judging by the way in which Mike speaks.

The following season saw Stoke continue to build on the experience of the previous year. This time they challenged on three fronts, the league, another extended F.A.Cup run and of course the League Cup run itself. The League Cup adventure of 1971-72 began with the trip to Southport. Whilst they felt supremely confident, little did they imagine that they would be the eventual winners. Pej played his part as one of five players who were ever-present throughout the run. But what are his memories of those games? "I didn't realise that I was ever-present until it was pointed out to me very recently. However as for memories, I remember that whilst we were quite fit, I picked up a knee injury, which wasn't really responding to the treatment I was getting from our physio Mike Allen. At that time, we were getting extra fitness training from Roy Fowler (the 10,000 metre runner) and he – unbeknown to the Stoke physio – manipulated my knee ligaments, which allowed me a good deal more mobility in the joint. Following the earlier games against Southport and Oxford United, we were once again pitted against Manchester United in another extended fixture, which we deserved to win. Then, as I recall, we travelled to the West Country to play Bristol Rovers at their Eastville ground. It was a ground that was surrounded by a dog track, which meant that the fans were well away from all the action. We felt this lack of atmosphere and were unsettled by it for the first couple of minutes, but once we got into our stride, we took control of the game and I knew that we couldn't lose that night. Then there was the semi-final against

West Ham United. We all had this feeling – which is hard to describe – that we couldn't lose; it was, I think, because we had been playing together as a unit and had a feeling of almost invincibility. Even after the ref. gave the penalty (which was caused by a mix-up between Gordon and myself), I couldn't see us losing. Banksie certainly repaid our faith in him as he made that world-class save from Hurst's penalty. It was a fantastic save and a great evening. After the disappointing game at Hillsborough, where the conditions were really against us (both teams), we went to Old Trafford and came away with a very

Pic. E Fuller

deserved victory. Each player, I felt, had a part to play in that victory and each man was certainly up to the task on that night".

After the semi-final victory, the build up for the final began in earnest. The lads were measured up for their suits, the mementoes were being produced and the squad went into the recording studios to cut the disc, "We'll Be With You" - the record finally charted at number 38 in the top 50 - but as Pej recollects: "The audition was funny as one or two of the lads were pulled away from the mike, obviously not hitting the right notes. Then we progressed to the week of the final itself and there was a subtle change to our preparations. As the week went on, it began to dawn on each of us that we were on the brink of creating a piece of club history, by being the first Stoke City squad to play in a Wembley final. On the Friday, the lads were quieter than usual and, as the butterflies set in, most of us just ate something light, such as egg on toast, or just toast, instead of the usual steak. Then came the day itself and the trip to the stadium. We were all gee-ed up for the game as the adrenaline flowed during the ride along Wembley Way; then the coach swept into the tunnel area and the large doors closed behind us. As I got off the coach, I looked through the doors and could see many of our fans. One in particular was gesturing to me. It was a lad who I had been to school with, who just wanted to wish me good luck! There was an air of expectancy in the dressing room as we got ready for the match. We all wanted to prove the national press wrong, as they had all been tipping Chelsea to be easy victors.

"As for the game itself, we went out with no more specific instructions than usual. However, I had read that the Chelsea boss (Dave Sexton) had told his players that he expected me to continue to play as normal, by overlapping and creating extra attacking opportunities and that they should be able to exploit the area that I would have left unattended. (Meeting him many years later, he told me that he never said anything like that at all), However, I took this on board and played less of an attacking role than I usually would have done. This ploy obviously worked, as Charlie Cooke had very little space that day. Looking back at the match, everything just seemed to fall into place at the right time. If we lost the ball, the midfield trio would drop back and help the defence. Both Bluto and Smithy were exceptional in the centre of defence. As for Banksie, well he was in great form and it was just an honour to play in front of him. He had an exceptional day as the save from Bernie's back-pass proved".

Just breaking away from his recollections of the day, Mike reflects the world-wide esteem that Gordon is held in, as he recounts a tale of a trip to Portugal a couple of years ago: "I was on a beach, just walking back toward our apartment, when I saw a man rise from his sun-lounger and walk toward me. Recognising me and with a broad grin spreading all across his face, he enquired about 'his good friend Gordon' – the man was none other than the legendary Eusabio!"

However, back to March 4th 1972 and Stoke City's Wembley dream, as Mike continues: "T.C's early goal really settled us and I was convinced that we would win. They scored a scrappy goal through Osgood, who was on the floor at the time. Then in the second half, as we were kicking toward our fans, George scored our second at a time which knocked them for six. The only other moment which caused us any real concern, was when Bernie played that rather rash back-pass. But Banksie was aware of the situation and he read the danger and got to the ball, preventing a Chelsea equaliser. I also remember the sight of Jackie Marsh scrabbling about on the grass looking for his 'other eyes'. As for the end of the match, it was all pretty amazing, there was the noise from all of our fans, but after a moment of euphoria, there was almost a feeling of anti-climax, as we realised that we had done it. Then there was the realisation that we had finally won a major trophy for our club. I'm sorry if this sounds a little confused, but we really were awash with an amazing amount of emotions all at once. For me, there was the realisation that I had at last kept the promise that I had made to both my father and grandfather many years ago, as I watched my first ever match, that one day I would play for Stoke at Wembley.

"After the match, we didn't really want to leave the ground. We wanted to jump into the crowd and celebrate with them. The next great memory for me was of the following day and the reception that we received as we drove from Barlaston through to Stoke Town Hall. Now that was fabulous!"

Following that glorious weekend, it was back to the normality of league football and Mike, even today, "feels disappointed that we could not really build on the success of the League Cup and for some reason, we were never really consistent and that's what we needed to gain more honours for the club". The following year saw Stoke play in Europe for the first time ever, when the club played Kaiserslauten; but, as Pej says looking back at Stoke's golden era: "I felt that we should have done better than we did, but it wasn't to be because there was a lack of thought put into the pre-match planning etc. We needed to address one or two issues to have become the complete side".

This became obvious in the 1974-75 season, as the Potters challenge for that elusive first division title faltered at Ipswich, when John Ritchie broke his leg. It was a season littered by injury, but despite this, they still pushed for the title. If the directors had been 'brave enough' and backed Waddo's judgement, and bought Frank Worthington, they surely would have won the league title.

However, it was not to be and the decline set in, as Waddo was forced to break-up this successful side following the collapse of the Butler Street Stand. Initially, Jimmy (Greenhoff) went to Manchester United and then Mike was transferred to

Everton. Ever the pragmatist, Pej went to Goodison, saying: "I remember that it was a great day of sadness for me! I also recall that Waddo said to me 'if I sell you, I will get the sack', prophetic words indeed! The ironic thing was that my first game for the 'Toffees' was at Stoke". Following his stint on Merseyside, Mike returned to the Midlands after Everton accepted an offer from Aston Villa. "My career with both Everton and Villa were shortened by injury. The last injury proved to be a major barrier and forced me to retire".

Pic. E Fuller

Apart from his club career, Mike played for both the under 23 and full England sides, gaining 8 under 23 and 4 full caps. (Surely this would have been a great deal more had Sir Alf Ramsey not have been sacked after the loss to Poland in 1974).

Mike moved away from football following his early retirement from the game and went back to school, albeit as an assistant sports teacher, before going into business on his own. However, his obvious coaching talents had been recognised and he re-entered the world of soccer, initially with Knypersley Vics, before moving to the Harrison Park home of Leek Town. He moved from the hot seat at Harrison Park up the footballing ladder to Northwich Victoria. " That was a great experience (at Northwich) which helped me when I moved to the Vale, initially as youth team coach and then with the first team as well. I was there for six years in total and really should have used it as a stepping-stone along the managerial route. However, being the person that I am, I put my loyalty to the club first, which in hindsight probably held me back".

After leaving the Vale, Mike worked for the Football Association's coaching staff for 18 months, before being offered the chance to coach in Kuwait on a twelve month contract, which he describes as being "a great experience". As the contract ended he returned to England to take up the managerial duties at Chester City in 1995, for most of a season which he also enjoyed, despite all the financial problems that the club were having. After he had rebuilt the side from scratch, the club was faced with another financial crisis and were forced to release Mike, which when you consider what he had achieved in such a short period of time, was a scandalous thing to do. Being the battler that he is, Mike did not take this lying down and duly bounced back. He was asked to coach in Australia; however ten days before his flight, Lou Macari contacted him and offered a job on the coaching staff at Stoke City. It was, as Mike says: "A dream come true; after all, I had played for the club that I had supported all my life and to be asked to return in a coaching role was something special indeed".

Following Lou's departure from the club, surely it would have been better had the board promoted from within, but this was not to be the case, as a succession of managers quickly followed. Mike's tenure as coach became more and more precarious, which disappointed him greatly. Indeed, it was so precarious that he was finally dismissed. A decision that created an emotion scar which is still evident to this day.

Once again, against all the odds, Pej bounced back to take another coaching role with the Football Association, during which time he has been seconded out to the Zimbabwean Football Association and then took up a coaching role in Malaysia. After a successful stint in the Far East, Mike returned to England and took up the role of the Football Association's North East Regional Director of Coaching, a role with which he was involved with the national squad. He has now moved back to North Staffordshire and is looking forward to seeing all his old friends and visiting the Britannia Ground, to see his team once again.

Pic. E Fuller

4

Pic. E. Fuller

Mike Bernard

Born in Shrewsbury on January 10th 1948, 'Bernie' is another product of the juniors. He joined Stoke after playing against the City of Stoke on Trent schools side. He made his 1st team debut in 1966 and played in every round of the League Cup run scoring two goals on the way.

This chapter has been kindly supported on behalf of Margaret Wood.

(Shropshire born), Mike Bernard joined Stoke City in 1961, having impressed both manager Tony Waddington and chief scout Cliff Birks in the English Schools Trophy match between the City of Stoke-on-Trent Schools and Shropshire Schools. This was despite his side losing their early 2 goal lead, by conceding 10 goals at Northwood Stadium; but why did he choose to join the Potters? Mike recalls that: "Tony Waddington pulled a masterstroke that created a great impression upon me. He invited both teams to watch Stoke play a league game that afternoon and after, he asking me into his office and introduced me to Jimmy McIlroy, Dennis Viollet and the great Stanley Matthews. This was a magical moment for me, it was like all the cigarette cards that I used to collect as a child suddenly coming to life in front of my very eyes. That really swung it for me, despite invitations from both Shrewsbury Town and Stan Cullis' Wolves, I had made my mind up to join Stoke". However, the move from Shrewsbury to the Potteries was not all plain sailing for the young Michael Bernard, as after two weeks in Stoke, he packed his bags and went home, suffering from homesickness. Arriving home, Mike remembers the welcome he got from his father as he begged him to get his contract with Stoke torn up. "He clipped me around the ear and, telling me not to be so daft, he packed me back off to Stoke. It is the best thing that he ever did for me and it is something that I will be grateful for, for ever".

Mike soon adapted to the apprentice lifestyle at Stoke, doing the chores in the morning and training in the afternoon. It was, as he recalls; "my responsibility to look after the dressing rooms and the senior players kit and boots". Indeed, he further recalls that: "the then 'hardman' of Stoke, Eddie Clamp, required his boots and studs in particular, to be cleaned and honed in such a way as to enable him to be able to 'stamp' his authority upon his opponents during the game". Mike made his 1st team debut for Stoke at Anfield playing on the right wing, wearing the legendary number 7 shirt that usually adorned the shoulders of the great Stanley Matthews. Mike explains: "It was toward the end of Stan's career and Tony was picking and choosing the games that he was to play in and this was one to avoid, as Tommy Smith would have been delegated as his marker. So there was I, some ten minutes into the game, as both Tommy Smith and 'Big' Ron Yeats clattered into me. Smith kicked me and Yeats stood on my head. Helping me to my feet, they both said 'welcome to the 1st division son.' To say the least it was a baptism of fire. I remember that the match had been televised and would be shown on the telly the following day. As we only had an indoor aerial, my girlfriend (now my wife) had to stand in the corner of the room, holding it at an angle so I could see myself on the telly for the first time ever". By the 'cup years', 1970-1972, 'Bernie' was an integral part of the midfield set-up at Stoke, which came as some surprise to the man himself as he says: "I was an attacking inside forward who scored a few goals, when Tony signed me and that's where I continued to play, until I was asked to move back into the midfield role which earned me my long-term first team place". As Mike looks back at his career in the midfield, he laughingly suggests that: "I may have been able to add another 4 to 5 years to my career had Tony not moved me back into the midfield slot with 'Pierre' and 'Skippy', as I had to do all the running around while they 'just' trapped the ball and then sprayed perfect 45 yard passes around willy-nilly".

Pic. E Fuller

As either a midfield dynamo or destroyer, Mike Bernard soon gained a reputation of being an exceptional talent, which didn't go unnoticed as he gained both youth and under 23 caps. His battles with Peter Storey in the F.A.Cup semi-finals were not for the feint-hearted. Looking back at those two years, Mike, like many Stoke fans, insists that " it wasn't only Arsenal who beat us; the referee didn't do us any favours either. He appeared to favour the London team. On the pitch he used to speak to them using their first names, while with us it was always Bernard this or Pejic that". This lack of judgement (for want of a better term) indeed manifested itself during both games, as several important decisions went Arsenal's way. Decisions, which it has to be suggested, cost Stoke two cup final places!

Mike was an ever-present during the League Cup run of 1971-72 and scored in the thrilling 2nd replay of the semi-final against Bobby Moore's West Ham United, on that rain-soaked night in Manchester. A goal which he recalls as the greatest moment of his footballing life:
" I played against Billy Bonds who was a very hard, but very fair player and thoroughly enjoyed the experience. Really, it was a clash of the titans, as neither of us would ever give ground. We lost the first game and were written off by the press as being cannon fodder for the 'Hammers' down there. That made us even more determined and we came away with a well-earned victory. The game at Hillsboro' was not the most aesthetically pleasing, but once again 'Bonzo' Bonds and I had a good tussle with each other. Then came the match at Old Trafford and the moment of madness, when I stepped up to take the penalty-kick against Bobby Moore, who had replaced the injured Ferguson in goal. Don't ask me why I grabbed the ball, because I'd never taken a penalty in my life. I think it was probably the adrenaline rush that got to me. However, there I was spotting the ball and walking back to the start of my run up. (It wasn't until we were back

at the Place later that night, that it really hit me what I had done). I hit the ball to Bobby Moore's right-hand side, having changed my mind as I ran up to the ball. He guessed correctly and managed to get his hands to the ball and push it back out. It came back to me and I (laughs) coolly slotted it past him with a left-footed shot. Amazingly, it was the only goal that I have ever scored with my left-foot, so you can imagine how I felt; and there we were – in a Wembley Cup Final for the first time ever". Mike, along with the other members of the squad and a number of invited supporters, made a record during the build-up to their first Wembley appearance. The song, "We'll Be With You", finally made the charts, entering the top 50 at number 38. However, it wasn't the recording of the song that Mike recalls, but rather an amusing event that occurred on the Tuesday prior to the game itself.

"It was our last night of 'freedom' and Waddo had arranged for us to visit the Surrey home of Jackie Trent and Tony Hatch (the composers of the record). There we were surrounded by gold records, being well-entertained and having one or two drinks, nothing really heavy. I had a brandy and remember that I put my glass down on the top of their grand piano and knocked it all over the keys. All I could think of was how much would it cost me to replace it if I had done some serious damage to the piano. However, I didn't do that much damage and both Tony and Jackie laughed the accident off".

What then of the match itself and the Wembley experience? Whilst most fans instantly recall the moment when Mike played the ball back to Banksie and nearly let Osgood in for the equaliser, they fail to recall or recognise the effort that 'Bernie' put in that day, as he recalls:

"Tony (Waddington) was worried about both Charlie Cooke and Alan Hudson and their ability to provide chances for Chris Garland and Peter Osgood. With this in mind, he detailed me to nullify Hudson's natural talent and this, I feel, I did to the best of my ability; but of that back-pass, I must admit that my heart was beating faster than normal as I saw Ossie running onto the ball. However, I realised that Banksie was alert to Ossie's run and sprinted out to spread himself in front of the ball, thereby denying the Chelsea man an equaliser".

What then is Mike's abiding memory of that amazing day?
"Apart from the result, obviously, the most amazing part for me was as we emerged from the tunnel and walked onto the pitch. The sight of a red and white sea greeted us as we saw our supporters at the far end of the stadium. It was fantastic. We had all heard the stories of how the pitch would have an effect on our legs toward the end of the game, but in all truth, I felt as though I could have run forever. As for the feeling when we ran around the stadium with the cup after the match, well, it was just so emotional".

So, Stoke City had finally won a major trophy, but as the fans made their way home to the Potteries, having sampled all the thrills, the Bernard family had a further moment of excitement later in the day. As the team celebrated at the Russell Hotel in the centre of London, Doreen, Mike's wife, went into labour. Alan Bloor's wife Sandra assisted them as they made their way to the hospital, where their daughter Kim was born on the Sunday morning. So Mike had a double celebration that weekend as he says:

"We arrived back at Barlaston and were driven into Stoke on an open-topped coach with the crowd getting larger each yard of the journey. An amazing sight greeted us as we arrived in Kingsway for the civic reception at the Kings Hall. After the reception I returned home and packed a bag. I returned to London the same day to collect both Doreen and Kim, which you could say was a magical end to a fantastic weekend for me". Bernie chuckled as he further recalled the headlines in one paper which read 'Stork City 3 Chelsea 1'.

Following the League Cup victory, the Potters returned to mount a challenge for another trophy that season, reaching a second successive F.A.Cup semi-final, where they once again came up against the mighty Arsenal and a referee! As in the previous year, it was not to be. It was just after this that the Everton manager Harry Catterick offered Stoke £140,000 for Bernard. Mike, who had made 177 first team appearances (and scored 11 goals), heard about this offer on a day off from training as he recalls:

"I was playing golf at Leek and was enjoying quite a good round, when the club pro called to me saying that Waddo wanted to speak to me, as Harry Catterick had made an offer for me. I thought he was playing a joke, so I finished my round before 'phoning Tony. I didn't really want to go to Everton and several of my team-mates didn't want me to go either, seeing it as the start of the breaking up of a strong side; but Stoke needed the money and I was on my way to Goodison". It was a cultural shock for Bernie as the bi-partisan feeling in Liverpool between the neighbouring clubs was intense. However, he once again proved his class as he recalls:

"The pressure to win was greater than at Stoke, however, it was more important to both the club and the fans that we should win the 'derby' games and finish above Liverpool in the league, than to actually win it. Looking back at that period of my life, I think that my lasting memory must be of the clashes that Tommy Smith and I had. They were built upon by the local press as to almost resemble a war and that's what they felt like! Apart from that, I got a lot of enjoyment playing alongside two of the country's best midfield players, Howard Kendall and Colin Harvey - what an experience! Week in, week out, there was a big match atmosphere, but during my time at Goodison, we never actually won anything". Injury curtailed Mike's career with the 'Toffees' and he spent much of his last season in the treatment room. Everton released him and he joined Oldham Athletic, but as he remembers:

"It wasn't the best time of my career as I was being passed by players who really shouldn't have been on the same pitch as me". Finally, injury put an end to Bernie's career and he was forced to hang his boots up. That, however, wasn't an end to his involvement in football. After he and his family had run a hotel in Chester for several years, football beckoned to him in the shape of Crewe Alexandra. He returned to the sport that he loves so much as the Alex's Football in the Community Officer. Later, he was promoted to work in the commercial department of the club and rose to the position of Commercial Manager. Today, Mike Bernard is still involved in the world of football, employed as a scout and has worked for several clubs including Manchester City and Swindon Town. Living in Wiltshire, he still visits the Potteries on occasions to see his family and has visited the new home of Stoke City, but wasn't very impressed with the atmosphere, as he says:

"It was for a LDV trophy match and I was there to watch a player from the visiting club, but I felt that there was a lack of atmosphere there, although in defence of the fans there were only 2500 in the crowd".

Pic. E Fuller

5

Pic. E. Fuller

Denis Smith

Born in Stoke-on-Trent on November 11th 1947, 'Smithy' is yet another product of the junior ranks. He originally signed amateur forms for the club in 1963 before turning professional in 1966. He made his 1st team debut away at Highbury in 1967. He played in 8 games during the League Cup run, scoring 1 goal in the quarterfinal. The cup run also saw Denis being made team captain for the first time.

This chapter has been kindly supported on behalf of Gill Pilcher.

Such was Denis Smith's determination to 'make the grade' with his beloved Stoke City that, following two successful seasons in the City of Stoke-on-Trent side which won the English Schools Shield, he rejected the professional terms offered by both 'Spurs and Portsmouth preferring to sign amateur forms for the Potters in 1963. Club director, Percy Axon, supported Denis' dream by giving him an apprenticeship with his company, Axon and Brown, which allowed him to train two nights a week and play in the youth team on Saturdays. He lasted twelve months with Axon and Brown before leaving to work – with his brothers and sisters at the Stone factory of Lotus shoes – as a 'clicker' for some 18 months. What I hear you ask is a clicker? We'll let Denis explain:

"Unlike Mick Starkey, Phil Weston, Bill Bentley, Jack Marsh and John Worsdale I wasn't offered pro. terms. However, Percy Axon gave me an apprenticeship which allowed me to train and play with the youth team. But I never liked taking orders, so after twelve months I left and became a 'clicker' at Lotus in Stone. What's a clicker? (laughs and continues) A clicker is a time-served trade where if you don't do it correctly you may lose a finger or two. You use an extremely sharp knife to cut through leather and animal skins during the shoe making process". Being left-handed presented a few problems for the young trainee as nobody had actually taught a 'leftie' before. Resisting all attempts to get him to swap hands, Denis soon learned the necessary skills and became quite proficient at the job. He stayed there for some eighteen months before finally being offered professional terms at the Victoria Ground.

His decision to sign for the Potters did, however, come at a personal financial cost to the young Denis, as he explains: "Financially I was better off staying with Lotus as I was being paid £20 a week because when I saw Tony (Waddington) after breaking into the reserve side he asked me how much I was earning and when I told him he said 'that there was no way that the club could afford to pay you that, I can only offer you £12'. Despite this drop in pay I knew that it was the right thing for me to do, so I duly became a full-time professional with Stoke".

The progression up the footballing ladder was a relatively quick one for the central defender. By 1967 he was a regular in the reserve side and was challenging for a first-team spot. His, almost single-minded, determination to make it in the professional ranks was more than evident in October 1967. This was the month in which he married his childhood sweetheart Kate. However – the reserves were playing Everton that afternoon. So what did he do? Denis takes up the story: "The decision to get married in the morning because I wanted to play in the afternoon, so I wouldn't lose my place in the reserves, against

Everton didn't really go down too well. But Kate has always supported me and in the end agreed to the morning service. Tony made me captain for the day, so that was an extra wedding present which meant a lot to me at that time. However, Everton weren't as generous as they beat us 3-0, with Joe Royle getting a hat-trick".

Denis' progression into the senior side suffered a slight set back when he broke a leg during another reserve fixture later in the season. However, he made the first team the following year as he and John Worsdale made their senior debuts at Highbury. He, rather amusingly, recalls his rise through the ranks, saying: "I think that the only reason I got into the first-team was because they didn't like playing against me during training. I once put 'Taffy' (Roy Vernon) over the touchline with a tackle that he didn't really like. He was the captain at the time and as such expected a certain amount of respect, he asked what was I doing. I answered that if he's playing he should get back on to the pitch and if not then maybe he should 'bugger off'. I didn't think that he should take the mickey out of me. From then on I wasn't allowed to play in practice games until I got into the senior side. Basically this was because they had told Tony that they didn't like playing against me so he had better play me with them in the 1st team and so I got into the side in 1968, making my debut along with John Worsdale against Arsenal".

Having made his debut and being acclaimed by the People newspaper as the man of the match, scoring 9 out of 10 in their form indicator, Denis proved to be a big hit with the fans as his partnership with Alan Bloor, in the centre of the Potters defence, went from strength to strength. "I was fortunate", Denis says,"having Bluto alongside me to sweep up anything that got past me allowed me the freedom to really attack the opposition and the ball. I knew that if anyone did get past me then he would get him. He never seemed to get booked despite the fact that he would probably trample all over them with his 14st., he would just say 'sorry' and get on with the game. We also 'talked' to the opposition in an attempt to dominate the game. I remember one game against Newcastle United at St. James Park, Bluto and I were marking Malcolm MacDonald and John Tudor. 'Supermac' challenged me as we both went for a high ball. Winning it quite easily I turned to Alan I said, 'he can't head can he?' A couple of minutes later I beat him to a long through ball and once again turned to Bluto, this time, saying 'the fat little sod can't run either!' John Tudor turned to us and asked 'will you two leave him alone'. This chat between players can help and it did that day as I recall, as Malcolm really had a 'stinker' ".

Denis' reputation as a hard, but fair, defender was well deserved. However, his style did present him with the odd problem here and there, as he suffered from the occasional fracture. On one such occasion, at home against Ipswich, he limped over to the dug-out ten minutes after being on the receiving end of a very strong tackle and said to the physio, "I think I'd better come off, I've broken my leg again". Looking back at those days Denis shrugs and says, "it's only pain and pain is relative to the situation that you are in at the time".

Three years after his first-team debut, Denis lined up in a F.A.Cup semi-final for the first time, as Stoke met Arsenal at Hillsborough. Like the many thousands of fans who travelled to Sheffield that day, he has clear memories of the events that prevented the Potters from reaching their first ever Wembley cup final. It must be said that we were robbed by the inadequacies of referee Pat Partridge. Stoke were winning 2-1 and it looked they had booked their place in the final, when suddenly there were an extra six minutes to be played. As Denis says; "We didn't know where the extra time came from but had to abide by the ref's. watch. He then gave a free kick against Pej. which should never have been awarded. They took it and Banksie was clearly fouled as he came for the ball but he (the ref.) didn't see that. As I fell the ball flew along the ground toward the net. I managed to punch it clear without being penalised (another foul missed by the ref.) for a corner. From the kick, the ball was deflected goal-ward, Josh dived at it and handled it clear. Partridge saw that and awarded the penalty. They equalised in the last seconds of the game which - to say the least - was very disappointing. Looking back at that decision, I think that that result really knocked our confidence as we never got into the replay the following Wednesday".

Stoke, however, duly bounced back from the disappointment the next season, as we all know, with the League Cup win and another F.A.Cup semi-final appearance against Arsenal to their credit. Denis played a significant part in the cup run and scored several memorable goals, including the one in the quarter final against Bristol Rovers at Eastville, but as he says: "I don't actually remember that goal against Bristol because I had a bang on the head from an earlier collision and ended up with concussion. What I do recall, though, is the match against Manchester United at the Victoria Ground. I wasn't fit to play as I had a back problem. However, we got stuck in traffic as Kate, my wife, drove us to the ground. I told her that I would walk the rest of the way, as I didn't want to be late. As I got out of the car I felt a 'click' in my back as the problem righted itself. I reported to the ground and told Tony that I was fit and he played me. I repaid his trust by scoring a goal, as I seem to remember".

Denis missed both the home and away legs of the semi-final against West Ham through suspension but returned to the side for the replay at Hillsborough and for what turned out to be the decider at Old Trafford. The match had its moments but for sheer excitement the final game, in a rain soaked, Manchester was one to be remembered by Denis: "It was tremendous 'theatre' on a typical English cup replay night –

Pic. E. Fuller

with the awful weather (I remember as we stripped-off after the game our feet were blue because of the cold). There was the penalty and Bobby Moore's save, it was pure magic". Unlike the others, Denis has been able to make sense of the Hammers decision to put Moore into goal following Bobby Ferguson's collision with T.C. "On the surface, it did seem a strange decision. However there may have been several reasons why such an influential defender went into goal. The first may have been that he was the only one who was prepared to do so. Or it may have been a pre-planned thing, should the 'keeper have been hurt. Certainly he proved his goalkeeping capabilities that night, as he parried Bernie's penalty-kick, despite the fact that he couldn't get to the rebound". So, after a thrilling 3-2 victory Stoke had finally made it to a Wembley final after a 108 year wait.

During the build-up to the final itself, there was the inevitable record. Denis is reticent about revealing the identity of those who weren't allowed to sing on the single but (laughingly) suggested that he may well have been one of them. After moving to their London hideaway the squad had their last night of 'freedom' at Tony Hatch and Jackie Trent's mansion, before concentrating on the more serious matter of the League Cup Final itself, Denis says: "I personally felt that the build-up was just right, getting away from Stoke allowed us to escape from the pressure. Despite being written off as the underdogs we were very confident and I think that showed, especially on the day! As we lined-up in the tunnel, I realised my childhood ambition of playing for Stoke at Wembley. I knew that we would not lose that day. We could see how tense they were as we stood alongside them in the tunnel and we all realised that the game was ours for the taking".

Onto the game itself, does Denis recall the events on the pitch? "Once Bluto bought Garland down in the first few minutes we felt very much in control. Then came the first goal after 5 minutes. Peter took a long throw and I flicked it on, I remember turning around and seeing Jimmy's shot rebounding to T.C. who headed it past their 'keeper. After that, Osgood stamped on my ankle and I had to play the rest of the match with a swollen ankle. I wasn't particularly pleased with him so I clattered into him a couple of times. Then there was Jack Marsh who as we lined up for a corner whispered to me 'Den. Den.' I said what's up, he replied 'I've lost my lens I can't see'. Oops! Hold on ref. (laughs) Then we saw him on the ground scrabbling around looking for it. Then there was Jimmy, who played for most of the match with a badly damaged shoulder, but his reaction to the cross that led to the second goal was purely instinctive. He hit his trademark half volley, which Bonetti parried and George hit the winner. Really it was fairytale stuff as he was the oldest player to play in a League Cup final. Then, in the last few minutes, there was Bernie's backpass which nearly let Garland in. I was the last man and he pushed it past me I thought what the hell are you doing? However, THE MAN! was there wasn't he? As usual Banksie, whose concentration levels were amazing, saw Garland running through and just sprinted out to block the ball and once again save our skins. Then, after the whistle went, we walked up those 39 steps and collected the cup and our tankards. It's what all kids dream about, isn't it? And there we were actually doing it. It was a fabulous moment and a memory that nobody can ever take away from you. Then there was the trip back the following day and the memorable reception that we received every inch of the way from Barlaston through to Stoke. It was a magical moment, especially as we went through the Meir. Bluto and I stood on the coach with the cup and there was no way that anyone was going to get it off us. We were born 100 yards apart and this was our patch so it was a very special feeling. I can still remember looking out at all the people, they were even on the roof of the library, it was just fantastic!"

Then it was back to normality as the Potters continued to challenge for a decent position in the league and possibly another cup final. However, Stoke were, for the second year running, drawn against Arsenal in the semi-finals. Having already tasted the Wembley atmosphere once that season they were determined to get to a second final that year. As in the previous season they were robbed, once again, by some diabolical refereeing. "This time the ref. failed to notice that

Charlie George was so far offside that he could have been having a pint with his mates on the terraces".

The final curtain fell on Denis' career at the Victoria Ground in 1982 when, following a loan spell at York City's Bootham Crescent, he joined the Yorkshire club as 1st team manager, taking Viv Busby with him as his assistant. Within his first season in charge, Denis managed to turn the fortunes of the club on its head. From a team that had conceded 98 goals and had to seek re-election the previous year – they finished 7th in the division. In his second year York won the 4th division title and broke all records by becoming the first side to gain over 100 league points, scoring 97 goals into the bargain. He built on their league success during his third season as they finished 7th in the, then, 3rd division. "It was a super club to be involved with as they gave me my first chance on the managerial ladder and, whilst they didn't want me to go, they understood the situation and allowed me to go to Sunderland when they came for me in 1987. I spent nearly 5 years at Roker Park having inherited a good squad, but little money, with players such as Eric Gates and Frank Gray. I also brought in Marco Gabbiadini from York City for £80,000. We won promotion in my first year and finished 10th in the league in my 2nd. Then, in the third year of my tenure at Roker, we finished 6th and got into the play- offs. We were up against our north-eastern rivals Newcastle United and drawing 0-0 at home – having missed a penalty in the last minutes, we were definitely the underdogs as we went up to St. James Park but we won 2-0. This meant another trip to Wembley for me. This wasn't as enjoyable as we lost 1-0 to Swindon Town. However, they were denied promotion by the league because of certain financial irregularities. Therefore we were promoted by default! Our 1st year in the premiership wasn't a great success as we were relegated. In an attempt to regain our premiership position I tried to rebuild the team and sold Marco Gabbiadini for 1.8 million (this didn't go down too well with our chairman as he had named his dog after our star striker). But the results didn't go our way and I ended up by getting the sack - this was after Sunderland had already refused Stoke permission to approach me for their, then, vacant managers job".

Denis made a swift return to the footballing world when he accepted the role of manager with Bristol City. It was an interesting period at Ashton Gate as he brought in the likes of Andy Cole, for £500,000. However, things between Denis and the committee soured somewhat so he left.

Following his stint at Ashton Gate, Denis moved to Oxford United. They just missed promotion during his first two years at the club. Then, following a lean spell in the middle of his third season in charge, the team won 15 of their last 16 games to finish 2nd in the league table and gained automatic promotion.

However, the club were rebuilding their Manor Ground stadium and were having financial problems so Denis had to sell players to balance the books. This, in retrospect did have its funny moments. One such – as Denis recalls; "Concerned the Northern Ireland international Jim Magilton - we'd just beaten Leeds United 3-2 at Elland Road and I had to sell him so that we could pay the wage bill thereby keeping the club going. The following Saturday we played Chelsea in the Cup and were losing 2-1, when we got a penalty in the last minute and Jim had been our regular penalty taker. The lad who took it hit the bar, so we were out of the competition and that miss (probably) cost us as much as we made out of the sale of Jim, as he would usually have scored and we would have progressed to the next round. Much the same happened the following season as I was forced to sell Matt Elliott and that really hurt. However we did get 1.7 million pounds for him. But he had a real talent and it had been a real joy to work with him. Despite having to balance the books on an almost annual basis I really enjoyed my time there. The people were nice and I enjoy working with nice people. But in the end, we ran out of money as we were still rebuilding the stadium. So, I did one final deal, which netted them £80,000, as I negotiated my move to West Bromwich Albion. I went to the Baggies and must have done something right as we finished in the highest position in the league than we had done for many years. I was also reasonably successful in the transfer market for them".

From West Brom. Denis moved back to Oxford for a second spell in charge at the Manor Ground. However, as he says; "You really shouldn't go back should you? I had let my heart rule my head though, so I said I'd stay until the end of that season and try to keep them in the division. We succeeded as we managed to avoid relegation. Having been successful with my short term goal of keeping the side away from relegation the chairman asked me to extend my stay there. I did so, despite having had surgery on an old neck injury. Much to my wife, Kate's annoyance, I returned after only two days' convalescence – instead of the prescribed two weeks".

This early return to the managerial pressure-pot had a short-term detrimental effect upon Denis' health, so he decided to take time out and resigned. After a short period of recuperation he was asked to talent spot for several clubs and visited other countries such as Denmark and France to watch potential players. He also did a little t.v. and radio work, before going 'somewhat' against his wife's wishes by returning to football as manager of Wrexham (on the anniversary of their wedding, when they should have been celebrating in Paris) as he says;
"For a club of this size, they have a fabulous set-up with a newly developed stadium and a purpose built training ground. It is something that I wanted from

each team and this was the first time I got it before I started rather than having to fight the board for these facilities. They also seem a genuine and friendly club. Indeed, as I said to Kate, it's like coming home! The people are very similar to those in Stoke – they are so friendly and its only half an hour or so from home, so we can visit at anytime. She has supported my decision, although I did have to resort to a certain amount of bribery, by buying her a car, to get her to agree to me joining Wrexham".

Looking back at a long career in football, there must have been many highlights, but which were his favourite moments? "There was my debut at Arsenal – when I gave away a penalty but was described as the man of the match and obviously there was the League Cup Final itself. There was also the game against Ajax where I scored at home and when we nearly won across there as I headed the ball down to Jimmy Robertson – who hit it just wide from 3 yards out (the prat). However, I will never forget the feeling as Bluto and I held the cup aloft on the coach as we made our way to Stoke through the Meir".

Brian Clough – who attempted to sign Denis on several occasions- provides the footnote for the amazing football adventure that Denis has enjoyed. Denis had been asked by his sister to take a young Irish trialist across to Nottingham to see Cloughie. Denis, who at that time was once again in plaster, agreed and arrived at the City Ground at the appointed time. "I was", he says, "told that he was on the pitch coaching the 1st team squad after they had lost the previous day against Spurs. So I wandered out to the touchline and stood supported by my crutches waiting for him to finish. Cloughie saw me and beckoned me onto the pitch, whilst still lambasting his defenders. Looking directly at Kenny Burns and Larry Lloyd and pointing at me he said 'I will only be satisfied when you can defend as well as him'". A sentiment that surely was echoed by most managers throughout the land!

Pic. E. Fuller

6

Pic. E. Fuller

Alan Bloor

Born in Longton on 16th March 1943, 'Bluto' was yet another local lad who made the grade at the Victoria Ground. He made his 1st team debut in 1961. He and Denis Smith formed a formidable partnership. He played in 11 of the games in the League Cup that season and scored the opening goal of the campaign at Southport.

This chapter has been kindly supported by Nick Hancock.

Alan Bloor, the quiet man at the centre of the Stoke City defence who had, what appeared to be, an almost telepathic playing relationship with Denis Smith, joined Stoke as a fifteen-year-old in 1958. He was offered an apprenticeship, as a joiner, in Burslem but the cost of the bus fare from his Meir home was prohibitive, so he chose to join the groundstaff at the Victoria Ground. In January 1960 Alan, having made such an impact for the Stoke youth team, was selected to captain the England youth team, at Newcastle's St. James Park, against the Scotland youth side.

"There were some exceptional players in that team like Martin Peters, Gordon West, Bobby Tambling, Frank Saul and my room-mate Terry Venables (who is the same today as he was then, his attitude and character is the same as it was then, he was such a confident person that it is little wonder that he went on to represent England at every level). So yes it was a great honour. But I don't remember much about it apart from the fact that it was a 0-0 draw. I didn't even remember that Alex Ferguson (the United boss) was playing against me, until someone told me that he mentions it in his book", Alan recalls.

Two months later Alan turned professional when he signed a pro contract on his 17th Birthday, as he says; "That was on the toss of a coin because there were so many good players to choose from. Cliff Birks the club's chief scout and Frank Taylor (deputising for Tony Waddington, who was in hospital at that time) signed me. That's how football can be, that's how close it can be between being signed or released to go elsewhere. I was lucky because I ended up having twenty great years as a professional, heaven only knows where I would have been had the coin landed on tails".

Bluto made his 1st team debut the following season playing consecutive games against Norwich City and Liverpool. They beat Norwich 4-1 and drew with Liverpool. Alan, who kept very few mementoes of his career, cannot remember which game came first. However he does remember that: "Ian St.John played and it was up to me to mark him and looking at the score I must have done a reasonably good job. Despite this I wasn't in the next game as Eddie Stuart returned to the 1st team. I think that at the time Tony (Waddington) was putting his faith in experience, so when Eddie was fit he played again".

So, when did Alan become an established 1st team player? "I don't think that you ever become a 1st team regular as for the first two or three years you are just in and out of the team until you have proved yourself to the boss. However, I think I really became an established 1st team player by either the 1964-65 or 1965-66 season. Then I formed the partnership with Denis and we went from strength to strength, but before that I had played alongside George Kinnell, Ron Andrews, Maurice Setters and Eric Skeels until Denis made the number 5 shirt his own".

From the terraces the central partnership of Denis and Alan looked to be almost telepathic, but was it? Alan replies: "Well, it wasn't really a telepathic partnership. However, we had a very good understanding because Denis was a very aggressive player - he'd run through a brick wall for Stoke - so I used to say you attack the ball and if you miss it then its up to me to sweep up behind you. That was how the partnership worked and I was happy to clear up after Denis. So the understanding was there. Not only did Denis and I have an excellent understanding but the whole defensive unit, being local lads, put their bodies on the line for the cause of Stoke City (their own club). I felt that being local meant that we had a greater empathy with the fans and that further spurred us on to a higher level of play, a thing that doesn't happen as much today, as most players don't have the same sort of long standing allegiance to a club as we did".

"Waddo was slowly rebuilding the Stoke side, replacing many of the players whom had been instrumental in their winning of the 2nd Division Championship. This reconstruction meant that it took time for the consistency that was

Pic. E. Fuller

necessarily required for us to challenge for the major honours. However, by 1970 all the pieces were in place and so began our golden era. Everything happened during the next two years, especially in the two cup competitions. There were the games against Huddersfield Town and then quite a few, as I recall, against Manchester United (in both the F.A. and League Cups) – now they were special matches. The thing that really sticks in my mind, during the cup runs especially, was the level of support that we received. We may not always have had the 40-50,000 crowds that United, Arsenal or Liverpool regularly got, but what we did have was a special sort of support, possibly it's because the club had been starved of success so they were as passionate as we were when we did become reasonably successful. The games themselves seemed to come and go but it was this passion that has stayed in my memory. We had a good rapport with the fans and vice versa".

"Then came the semi-finals against Arsenal. Even now, some thirty years later, I still think that we were robbed of the rightful victories that we deserved. I am convinced of it. Okay, referees made mistakes then and they still make them today! But I will never understand how the referee or linesman didn't see the push on Banksie, when everybody else in the ground clearly could. I also don't know how or where he got 6 minutes of injury or stoppage time from because I can't remember any major injury or stoppage during the game, But that's referees for you isn't it? Then, the following year there was the incident with Charlie George being some 20 yards offside and neither of the officials saw him. At the end of the day, it was those two decisions" (or should that read 'refereeing errors') "that cost us two more Cup Final appearances".

Then, of course, there was the League Cup run itself with Alan setting the ball rolling as he scored the first goal of Stoke's campaign at lowly Southport. "I played a one-two with Jimmy Greenhoff on the edge of the box, then I just closed my eyes and slotted the ball into the back of the net. It was a good one-two, then again Jimmy was good at that anyway", Bluto recalled. Missing the game at Oxford, the big man returned for the replay at the Victoria Ground. It was a game that brought back a few memories for Alan. Then came the, almost inevitable cup-tie against Manchester United which went to a 2nd replay, once again at Stoke, before it was decided. Alan says that: "I remember that I marked George Best and did quite a good job. I also recall the reaction of the crowd, once again, as they really got behind us that night which, being a local lad, meant a lot to me. We then went to Bristol Rovers on a thoroughly wet night and the only thing I can remember was, as we got off the coach, we saw several of our regular supporters, many of whom I recognised, and signing a few autographs before going into the ground I knew that once again we couldn't let them down.

We didn't either, as we took the game by the scruff of the neck and beat them 4-2". Progressing into the semi-final Alan had a change of partner in the centre of the defence with both Jock (Stuart Jump) and Alfie (Eric Skeels) playing while Denis was missing. "We were very disappointed to lose the first game 1-0", Alan says, but of the second leg he recalls: "That was a magical result really, I well recall that the penalty was a result of a mix-up between Gordon and Pej. Hurstie took the kick and (excuse the pun) hammered it to Gordon's right. Banksie made an amazing save. Having dived slightly early he had to readjust his body, to beat the ball away with his forearms. Usually I am not the sort of person who lets his emotions show

Pic. E. Fuller

but I just picked him up and hugged him that night, because of the relief I suppose. After all, had the ball gone in we would have been out of the competion. Then we played the 1st replay at Sheffield Wednesday's ground and really it was a non-event. Following that it was on to Manchester United's Old Trafford for the game which had everything, despite the awful conditions. What with Bobby Moore going in goal after Ferguson had been injured (a decision which I still to this day cannot understand – managers make these silly decisions at times and this was one of momentous proportions) it worked in our favour. After all, to take the world's best defender and play him in goal was really just handing the match to us on a plate!"

Apart from the obvious weakening of their defence, the two main strikers – Geoff Hurst and Clyde Best - hardly got a look-in that night. "Yes we did very well", said Alan as he continued, "not just Denis and myself but the entire defensive unit was solid, you see we actually had an extra defender in Banksie. He would talk us through the game, he played the 'keepers role more as a defender. He would read the situation and tell us to go left or right and to hold or tackle, which is what you do at the back and that's the difference between a great 'keeper such as Gordon and lesser 'keepers. That was the difference between Gordon and Peter Shilton who was also an excellent 'keeper. They were both great but Gordon was also a 'natural' whereas Peter had to work at it".

Having got to the final, the squad entered the build-up phase by recording a single. Alan remembers that they went into the studio to lay down the vocal tracks with Tony Hatch and Jackie Trent, when he describes what happened: "We went into the studio and started to sing, however Tony (Hatch) walked round and tapped several of the lads on the shoulder and holding his fingers to his lips he indicated that they should just mime, as they were either tone deaf or just out of tune. I think Jackie Marsh was one of them".

"We left for London, by train, on the Tuesday and stayed in a hotel on the outskirts of the capital. However, while it was very comfortable, I couldn't really wait for the Saturday to come. Then, on the actual day itself, I was probably more nervous than any of the other lads in the squad. But in all reality it was just a brilliant day. What then do I remember of the day? Well, firstly there was the walk from the

Pic F. Fuller

tunnel and the sight of the mass of red and white that greeted us from the far end of the stadium. As we walked out I glanced across at the Chelsea players who, unlike us, appeared to look tense, nervous and worried. I can't say which for certain but, by then, we were a lot more relaxed. As for the match itself, it was over in a flash, but there are certain bits that I remember. I was booked in the first five minutes for a tackle from behind, I tell Banksie that I had to do it because if he had got through he would probably have scored. (In this day and age I would have been sent off for a similar offence.) Anyway we knew, in those days, that whatever we did in the first 5-10 minutes we would probably get away with it. Another thing that I recall was John's brilliant goal! But it was disallowed. Then Ossie scored. I remember that I mis-kicked the ball and Peter – who was on the floor at the time - scrambled it past Banksie. Yes! we'll put that one down to me I think. Then there was the moment of madness from Bernie as he made that back-pass and Banksie making that tremendous save. I also think that it was very fitting that George should have sneaked the winning goal. Then Norman Burtenshaw blew the whistle and the celebrations could begin! We had that amazing walk up the 39 steps to the Royal Box to collect the cup and our tankards. I remember that after the anthems we walked down to our 'end' of the ground and I stopped and pulled a couple of the others over and we stood and clapped our fans. We did this because we had the best fans in the land and we wanted to say thanks to them. After all, they had been behind us through both the lean and better times and they had suffered more than most because we had never won anything before. So, as this was the first thing that we had won, it seemed only right to include them in our celebrations".

"That wasn't the end of the weekend's excitement for the Bloor family, as on the Sunday morning after the game my roommate, Mike Bernard, woke me in an agitated state. His wife Doreen had gone into labour and was being rushed into the hospital and he wanted my wife, Sandra, to go with them. I remember that I was the one who really benefited as they went just before room service arrived, so I ended up having two breakfasts. Mike arrived back with the news that he was a dad for the second time, just before we were due to make the return journey. Then there was the journey back to Stoke. The train made a special stop at Barlaston allowing us to get off. We got onto the coach, it was an old banger which had seen better days as I remember, but it was the only one they could get which had an open top. We couldn't believe the amount of people that had come to Barlaston to see us. From Barlaston through to Meir Heath the crowd just got larger and larger. I must admit that there was the occasional tear in the eye. Especially for Denis and myself as we past through the area that we came from. It really touched me because the road from Meir Heath down to Broadway just stretched out in front of us and all we could see were the red and white clad fans and this is something that will live for me for the rest of my life".

Having returned home it was back to the nitty-gritty of a league campaign and, of course, the little matter of another cup run. Once again Stoke managed to battle through to the F.A. Cup semi-final where they, almost inevitably, were destined to meet Arsenal once again. "Yes, our friends Arsenal again – aided and abetted once again by some more unusual (to say the least) refereeing decisions. There was nothing we could do about it and it still goes on today. In cup matches you need some luck and once again that seemed to desert us against Arsenal".

The following year saw Stoke venture into Europe for the first time as they had entered the UEFA Cup as a result of the League Cup win. They were drawn to play the German club Kaiserslauten. The 1st leg was at Stoke, with the 2nd being in Germany. Alan recalls an incident in Germany that rather amused him, saying: "I was substituted during the 2nd leg with Reg (John Ritchie) replacing me. As I walked round to the dressing room I wasn't really watching the game, so I was rather surprised to be joined by John for the last few yards of my walk. What are you doing here, I asked, he replied 'I've come to join you!' I hadn't realised that he had been sent- off".

Alan's 18-year career with Stoke included a total of 484 first team appearances, in which he scored 19 goals. But can he remember those goals? "You would have thought so but I can only remember a couple that I scored against Manchester United. One was in a 1-0 'thrashing' of the 'Red Devils', which actually cost them the championship that year – as Brian Greenhoff reminds me whenever we bump into each other, I always reply that I am very pleased about that. The other was in a 1-1 draw, which came about from a cross by Kevin 'Bomber' Sheldon which Denis headed down to me and I volleyed it in, that was the best one I have ever scored. Obviously the third one that I can remember was the one against Southport".

"I actually left Stoke on bad terms because Alan Durban and I didn't see eye to eye. One thing that really upset me was that I was told, several months after leaving, that Durban told the board that he had offered me the youth-team coaching job and I was supposed to have turned it down. As I said to the club director who told me this, do you really think that I would have turned down such an opportunity after I had been with the club for so long? However, after a few months away from football I crossed the city and joined Port Vale and had two very good years there. Initially, as a player and youth/reserve team coach. I only played about half a dozen games for them because of injury. I did score one goal though! It was against the Alex, as I recall. I was lucky enough to coach youngsters such as Trevor Dance, Kenny Beech, Phil Sproson and the Chamberlain brothers. Then Dennis Butler was sacked and I was promoted over the Assistant-Manager, Graham Hawkins, to the position of manager. I thought this was wrong and so it proved, as two months later I resigned, following a game against York City where we lost 4-1. Looking back, I feel that the best thing that I ever did for that club was to offer the most talented youngster that I have ever come across to his first professional contract and after talking to his parents Mark Chamberlain duly became a Vale player. As things weren't working out I walked away from a life in football and into a world of commerce. For the next twelve years I had a furniture business in Longton, until we had to move because of the 'D' road. I then had a newsagents but to be honest it didn't agree with me so I retired".

Today Alan, who still lives in North Staffordshire, is still 'into' sport, however it is the sport of kings that is his real interest. He is also a very proud family man and is rightfully proud of his grandchildren. Obviously, he still looks for the results of 'his' club and regularly keeps in touch with his old team-mates. When pushed about his lasting memory of a lifetime in the world of football, Alan quickly says: "Without a shadow of a doubt the winning of the League Cup and the reception that we got on our return to Stoke has to be the highlight of my career".

Pic. E. Ful

7

Pic. E. Fuller

Terry Conroy

Born in Dublin on October 2nd 1947, 'T.C.' joined the Potters in March 1967 from the Irish club Glentoran and made his 1st team debut in October of that year. He played in 11 of the 12 matches during the League Cup run and scored 3 goals, including the first in the final itself.

This chapter has been kindly supported by Alec and Jo Bohannan.

Born into a large Dublin family (8 boys and 2 girls) Gerrard Conroy grew up, as did most boys of that time, with a football at his feet. His talents were recognised at an early age (10) when he was signed for the top junior side Home Farm. Within a year, he was playing in their under-13 side. This advancement continued as he developed because he always played at a more senior age level. Indeed, it was whilst he was at Home Farm that he won his first medal when they won the Irish Youth Cup. As he progressed, he would play on a Saturday for the senior side and on a Sunday for the juniors. "By the time I was 17, I had started to attract the attention and recognition from people outside of the Home Farm set-up. I even gained an Irish Youth Cap. As an 18 year old I was no longer eligible for the youth side but had become a regular in the seniors. We were quite successful and managed to get to the Leinster Cup Final. Having beaten Bohemians in the quarters and then St.Patricks in the semis, we met Dundalk in the final itself at Dalymount Park, the old international venue, and we won!."

This level of success, which can be likened to our League Cup competition, brought about the inevitable interest from clubs both north and south of the border. Being ambitious, the young Conroy had set his heart on playing in England, so in reality the offers from other clubs within the Republic really fell on 'deaf ears'. A representative from Glentoran visited T.C's parents and persuaded them - and him - that it would be the best way forward for the young Dubliner if he were to join them. After some consideration T.C. duly made the informed decision to join Glentoran, a team with a higher profile that would, hopefully, give him the opportunity to impress a club in England. "I signed for Glentoran and as a part-time professional was paid the princely sum of £6 per week, plus bonuses. However, what I didn't realise was that the club was going through a transitional phase, with several of the more experienced players moving onto other things".

As with any newcomer to a team, Terry had to prove himself and this was no exception as he started in the reserve or B team. However, as the man himself recalls; "I didn't know it but the team had reached the final of the 'Steel and Son' trophy, which was to be played the week after I had signed for the club. So there I was, after just one game, playing in a final against Larne. The final was on Christmas morning, with an 11.00 a.m. kick-off, at the Crusaders ground – and we won!" Looking back, the achievement of winning a medal within one week of joining his new

Pic. E. Fuller

club amuses the softly spoken Dubliner, especially when he recalls that; "After the match I had a four hour journey home to Dublin and was finally tucking into my Christmas dinner at 5 pm. that evening". Unlike England, there were no games on Boxing Day. However, that evening he received a telephone call from the club secretary, Billy Ferguson, informing him that he would be making his 1st team debut the following day in Belfast against Ards. Meeting up at the ground he remembers that he was introduced to his new team-mates for the first time (an occurrence that would happen again later on in his career). He made an instant impression in the senior side as he created the first two goals and scored the winner, in this, his 1st team

Pic. E. Fuller

debut. T.C. remained in the side, finishing the season with 24 goals to his credit and an appearance in the Irish Cup Final against Linfield. As in Glasgow, there is a 'divide' between the bitter rivals of Glentoran and Linfield, with the majority of the Glentoran supporters being Celtic fans whilst the Linfield fans were staunch Rangers fans. Despite this, T.C., playing for Glentoran, was playing with both Protestant and Catholic alike. Whilst, in reality, the Linfield side would never include a Catholic in its side. The match itself took place at the Oval, in front of a partisan 30,000 crowd, and as Terry modestly remembers; "We won 2-0 and I scored both goals".

Continuing to impress, the young Dubliner was gathering a host of admirers, including the Fulham boss Vic Buckingham, as well as the manager of Ards. Indeed, Buckingham had tabled an offer of £10,000 to Glentoran for Conroy just before their cup tie against Derrry. "I met with Mr. Buckingham to discuss my personal terms. To me, he was a bit like an Arthur Daley type figure and, while he was upfront and o.k. with me, I felt a little uneasy about the whole situation. Added to that was the fact that I didn't really want to go to London anyway, so I asked for a little time to think the move over". Glentoran were pressing T.C. for an answer, as £10,000 was a lot of money to the club. But having drawn the cup tie they really wanted him for the replay, so were happy to give him a little more time. This was in February 1967 and on the Wednesday of the replay he travelled north to Derry. However, the game fell foul of the weather as it had snowed and was consequently postponed. "Feeling that I had wasted a journey, I returned home via Belfast's Victoria Station. Waiting for the 2.00 p.m. train I was more than a little surprised to bump into the Ards manager George Eastham snr. He said, 'Hello Terry'. To which I replied, 'Hello Mr. Eastham'. He said, ' I've got someone here who would like to meet you, - Tony Waddington the manager of Stoke City'. I said, 'how are you?' Waddo joined in the conversation by asking, 'Would you mind if I joined you on your journey back to Dublin'. 'Sure', I replied, 'no worries about that'. Waddo explained, during the homeward journey, that he had come specifically to see me play that day, on the recommendation of George Eastham snr., who had intimated that he would be mad to miss such an opportunity. During the trip, Waddo convinced me that Stoke would be the best team for me to join. However, before a deal could be struck, I explained that he would have to speak to my parents, as parental agreement was needed because of my age. So I invited him home to meet my parents and he readily agreed. I introduced him to my parents and my father offered Waddo a drink (laughs) then they spent some time with a whiskey bottle between them, talking about everything but me. Waddo made such an impression on my father that he quickly agreed that Stoke would indeed be a good place for me, so a deal was struck, without the knowledge of Glentoran! I must add".

Because of the Fulham offer Waddo then had to go through the official channels by making Glentoran an offer for T.C.'s signature. He contacted them saying that Stoke would not only match the fee agreed by Fulham but would also play a game in Ireland against them with Glentoran keeping all the gate receipts. As T. C. recalls; "The exact fee turned out to be £15,000, which consisted of an initial fee of £10,000 with an extra £2,500 should I play 20 or more 1st team games and a final payment of £2,500 if I ever got a full cap, plus the money that was made from the game. So, all in all, Glentoran did rather well out of the deal in the end". The deal was done and Terry duly travelled to the Victoria Ground intent on signing for the Potters.

Looking back at the day that he signed for Stoke he remembers that it was a bit like an Irish joke, as he explains; "When I saw my contract, I pointed out that I couldn't sign it as it would not be binding. Bill Williams and Tony looked aghast, they couldn't understand what the problem was. I had to point out that they had made it out in the name of 'Terry' Conroy and not Gerrard, which is my real name. After explaining that, I was called 'Terry' by the family to differentiate between me and my uncle, (who I was named after) it had stuck throughout my life. So the contract disappeared and came back having been altered. I signed the changed document and duly became a Stoke player. A move that I have never regretted".

Making his 1st team debut in October 1967, Terry soon made the number 7 shirt his own. Indeed, he quickly passed the 20 game mark and Stoke made the second payment of £2,500 to Glentoran for the flame-haired Irishman. Following a series of impressive outings, Terry soon attracted the attention of the Irish team manager and was called into the full international squad to travel to Prague to play Czechoslovakia. Like the day he signed for Stoke, this experience also turned into something that resembled an Irish joke that was being played on Terry, as he remembers; "We, Stoke, had a game on the Tuesday night prior to the match in Czechoslovakia and I had been given permission to travel to Prague on the day of the game. Arriving at Prague airport, I found that I hadn't got the relevant entry visa and the officials wouldn't let me in the country. After some frantic 'phone calls, an official from the Irish F.A. arrived at the airport to sort out the problem and I was then allowed into the country. When we arrived at the hotel I booked in and was told by the official to go to my room and introduce myself to my room-mate, I did so – fully expecting to be sharing with someone I knew such as Paddy Mulligan or Steve Heighway or even the legendary Johnny Giles. So, imagine my surprise as I walked into the room to be greeted by a total stranger. 'Hi, I'm Terry Conroy'. I said introducing myself to the stranger. Looking up, he smiled and replied; 'Hi, I'm the Captain of the Aer Lingus flight that flew the side from Dublin'". Seeing the funny side of the meeting T.C. couldn't help but laugh at the situation. Now, with less than two and a quarter hours to the kick-off he still hadn't met his team-mates but this didn't unduly concern Terry as he expected to be there to make up the numbers. As the team had already left for the stadium, Terry was driven to the ground and ushered into the dressing room. The manager, however, informed Terry that he would be playing from the start and then introduced him to his new, international colleagues for the first time.

Terry, by the 1970-71, season was an integral part of the team that Waddo had built. Indeed following the return of 'Big' John Ritchie and the signing of Jimmy Greenhoff (both in 1969) the team almost picked itself, with the twelve men who participated in the final being the nucleus of that squad. T.C. remembers; "There was a family atmosphere within the club and, whilst there was an age gap between certain team members, it made no real difference to us as we were one big happy group. There were no prima-donna's in the team at all". Indeed, the Potters had become a team to be reckoned with, as they got to the F.A. Cup semi-final, only to lose because of what can only be described as a serious flaw in refereeing standards and T.C. had played his part in this rise of fortunes. Then came the 1971-72, season a year which brought about a new optimism and self-belief amongst the entire club. It had an effect on everyone, they were all determined to erase the memory of that semi-final debacle and so it proved during the League Cup run.

Terry, who had been attracting the attentions of other clubs (indeed Bill Shankly had made an offer well in excess of £100,000 for the talented Irishman), more than played his part in the cup success. He missed the first game at Southport but played in each subsequent game, scoring goals in the quarter final win over Bristol Rovers and the decisive goal in the epic semi-final struggle before scoring the opening goal in the Wembley final, itself. What did those goals mean to him? Terry once again takes up the story; "Thinking back, I can't remember much about the goal at Bristol but the goals at Old Trafford and Wembley are unforgettable. The semi-final was a great game to play in, it was full of incident. There was Hurst's penalty in the first leg, Reg's goal and Banksie's great save in the second leg at Upton Park. The immense cold at Hillsborough when we seemed to be camped out in their penalty box for the majority of the game. Then came the excitement of that wet, Wednesday night at Old Trafford. The memory of Hillsborough and Villa Park from the previous season spurred us on that night, we were determined not to lose and so it proved to be as we won 3-2 and I got the winning goal. (laughing and tongue in cheek) It was what Waddo had bought me for wasn't it? To score all those important goals. To me, it was the fulfilment of a dream. I had scored the goal that got us to Wembley, that night was special. It was a game that had everything but the relief of getting through was tremendous. I suppose then, when summarising the semi-final goal, that it was more what it meant than the actual scoring of it that is

Pic. Courtesy of The Sentinel

what I will always remember. Then, there was the goal in the final itself and what is definitely my most abiding footballing memory, seeing my name on the scoreboard at Wembley. In no way could it be described as a classic but from the floated centre the ball finally bobbled out to me and I headed it past a flat-footed Peter Bonetti into the back of the net. What really makes it memorable was the fact that I had realised a lifelong dream by scoring in a Wembley final. I was able to look up at the scoreboard and see my name in lights, it said: - Stoke City 1 Chelsea 0. Conroy '4. I almost had to pinch myself into believing that I wasn't dreaming".

"Whilst the rest of the match was something of a blur, as was the lap of honour, what I do really remember and it will be another everlasting memory, was the welcome home that we received on the Sunday. The crowds were fabulous, but what really made it memorable was seeing the reaction of the local lads, Smithy,

Bluto and Jackie Marsh, as we were driven through Meir and Longton (their home patches) to the town hall at Stoke and seeing what it meant to them".

Off the field T.C. was planning his own special 'match of the day' in 1972 as he and his fiancée Sue were getting married. Career-wise, Terry continued to play for Stoke until 1978. However, the latter days of his career at Stoke was blighted by a series of cartilage problems. Indeed, he actually had five operations, which caused problems to the way he played. In 1978 he left Stoke and went first to Crewe Alexandra before travelling to the far east to play in Hong Kong for Bulova, until he finally hung up his boots. He moved back to his adopted home in North Staffordshire to work in the commercial sector. However, the call of football was too great and he can now be seen at the Britannia Stadium, where he works in Stoke's commercial and marketing department and as he says; "I'm still able to involve myself with my team – Stoke City".

Pic. E. Fuller

8

Pic. E. Fuller

Jimmy Greenhoff

Born in Barnsley on 19th June 1946, 'Jimmy' joined Stoke City in August 1969 for a fee of £100,000 becoming the club's most expensive player. The former Leeds United and Birmingham City striker soon became the darling of the Boothen End and formed an almost telepathic partnership with 'Big' John Ritchie. Jimmy played in all 12 games during the League Cup run and scored 3 goals.

This chapter has been kindly supported by Phil Rawlins.

Stoke City's first £100,000 player was yet another product of the schools system who progressed through to the professional ranks. He recalls:

"I was fortunate enough to play in a Barnsley Schools side that seemed destined to play in the English Schools Shield final and this was a great stepping stone to the county side. I remember that we (Yorkshire) played against Lancashire – in a traditional 'Roses' battle at Blackpool. They were far superior to us on that day and beat us 6-2 (or 3). In a strange sort of way losing also proved to be a lesson that helped my future professional career". Following that, Jimmy signed for Don Revie's Leeds United. But why Leeds? "At that time, in Yorkshire, there were usually only one of three ways to go once you left school. The first was to go down the mines. The second was to go into the steel industry in and around Sheffield. Or you were called up for national service. However, it was actually my father's decision that I should go to Leeds United. He had been a useful player himself, having played for Lincoln City, and had a sneaking admiration for both Syd Owen, the Leeds coach and Don Revie, the Leeds boss. He thought that Syd would be a great coach and that Revie was a very good manager and so it proved over the years. So I signed for Leeds in 1961 and spent the next seven years at Elland Road".

During that time Jimmy was in and out of the side, never really gaining a regular 1st team place as he contested the wing-half position with the likes of Billy Bremner and Norman Hunter, among others. However he did play in 94 games and scored 21 goals.

"That wasn't such a bad record for someone who played at either wing-half or on the wing was it?"

Amongst those 94 games were winning appearances, in both the League Cup Final against Arsenal and then the 1st leg of the Inter Cities Fairs Cup Final, against the Hungarian side Ferencvaros. What does he recall of those occasions? "I didn't think I would be fit for the League Cup Final against Arsenal, as I had picked up an injury and needed a lot of treatment in between times. My injury had not responded and by the Thursday I felt that there was absolutely no chance of me playing, but, on the Friday morning I felt great and was able to join up with the rest of the squad. The rest is history; Terry Cooper scored after about 13 minutes and, for the rest of the match, I played as an extra fullback, bolstering our defence, so in all reality, I didn't enjoy the game. As for the Ferencvaros game, I must admit I'm still disappointed in the way that Leeds treated me. In those days that final was played over two legs and I'd played in the 1st leg. But in between that and the 2nd game, I was transferred to Birmingham City, for £70,000. As a result of this move, Leeds never gave me the medal that I was entitled to and in a way, it still rankles to this day. My move to Birmingham was brought about because I wanted to play regular 1st team football and, at that time, my chances at Elland Road were limited. So I made a move, which in hindsight, was really a mistake". Looking at the figures in an impassionate way, it is hard to see why Jimmy views the move to St. Andrews as a mistake, as in only 36 games, he scored a more than creditable 15 goals. But, as he explains:

"As I have already said it was a big mistake, I had moved down a division to get a regular 1st team place and as you have already indicated, I did manage to get 15 goals in 36 games. But, what you must realise, is that I actually got 12 of them in my first 9 games. Then, all of a sudden Stan Cullis, their manager, called me into his office and said that he wasn't happy with me. In all honesty I thought he was joking, as he had quite a dry sense of humour. But he wasn't, he was saying that I wasn't scoring enough goals. This seemed ridiculous to me, having scored 12 in 9 games, especially as I was really more of a provider than an outright goal-scorer. This upset me and I told him I wasn't going to play for Birmingham again, but obviously, because of my contract I had to. In the end, they finally agreed to let me go at the end of that season. Fortunately, Stoke came in for me and I joined them in August 1969".

Jimmy joined Stoke just in time for their pre-season tour of Holland, for a £100,000 fee. The question therefore must be; did being Stoke's first £100,000 player put any undue pressure on him? "Not really, but what made it easier was the fact that Everton also approached me; however Tony (Waddington) had already sold the club to me and, despite the fact that they had such players as Ball, Harvey and Kendall and the further fact that they actually went on to win the old 1st division title that season, doesn't change my mind as I look back. I'm sure I made the right decision!"

Jimmy went on to form a truly great partnership with 'Big' John Ritchie over the next few years, which, when added to the talents within the other areas of the team, led to Stoke's concerted challenge for the major honours during the next few years. This included the F.A. Cup run in 1970-71 and the League Cup win the following season. Can Jimmy explain the strengths of that striking partnership and why it worked so well? "I realised from an early stage that John had to score goals, otherwise he felt he wasn't performing as well as he expected. I think in the back of his mind he set himself targets and, if he didn't achieve them, he definitely wasn't a happy person. Whereas I was more of a provider, a throwback to my wing-half days I suppose. So in reality, this was how it worked so well. But looking back, there were the odd occasions when I possibly should have been a little more selfish, but I wasn't and the partnership went from strength to strength during that period. Looking back, I know that I was influenced by the late, great, Stan Matthews. I'd seen him on television in the 1953 Cup Final and decided that was how I wanted to play; after all, he was a provider and so was I".

Then came the League Cup run and the final victory after a 108-year wait. Jimmy played in all twelve games and scored three goals, one against Southport. The second, against Oxford and the final one in the quarter-final tie against Bristol Rovers. However, this wasn't his only contribution, as he set up the opening goal of the cup run for Alan Bloor. What are his memories of that night and of the cup run itself? "It was important for us to succeed against Southport. Not just because it meant we would progress to the next round of the competition, but also because it meant we were coming of age. That is to say, we used to play well against the larger clubs, but, for some reason, failed to perform against sides that we should have beaten week in and week out. So, looking back, it gave us the platform from which we were able to build a successful campaign. As for the first goal, it came as something of a surprise that Alan (Bloor) played a one-two with me, before hitting the ball into the net. It was something I feel he should have done more of. He was a lot better player than most people gave him credit for - not only in defence, but he could also play a bit and in my opinion, was unlucky not to have won any international honours. I was lucky to score the winner against Southport and then the goals against Oxford and Bristol Rovers - which to me were more important, as I have already said, it (for some unfathomable reason) was more difficult for us to beat the lower clubs, than to have scored against Manchester United or West Ham".

Pic. E. Fuller

Next came the epic semi-final struggle against West Ham United - a cup tie which was to stretch over four memorable games, culminating in that extraordinary match at a rain-soaked Old Trafford. What then are Jimmy's memories of those occasions? "I remember the trip down to West Ham. Mike

Bernard and I sat next to each other smoking - as we did in those days. It was the first time I saw Mickey as concerned as he was. 'I'd give anything for us to win', he said to me, 'Don't', I said, 'I've been dreaming about it all night'. The atmosphere in the dressing room was more intense than usual as we were so determined. I also remember Banksie and that save. It was the first time I ever had a prayer answered! I had to come off during the third game at Hillsborough and well remember sitting in the bath hearing a great cheer. I waited for the door to burst open and for someone to come in and tell me we were leading, but they didn't. So I was very relieved to be told that we had drawn, as I would be available for the 2nd replay. The final game at Old Trafford doesn't need commenting on, does it? It had everything, but what I still cannot understand, is why they put Bobby Moore in goal. That won us the match didn't it? It just played into our hands".

Pic. E. Fuller

Having got to the final, there was the usual build up and the inevitable record that went with it. Jimmy's contribution was heroic in the final, as he was on the receiving end of an awful tackle by Osgood and suffered a damaged shoulder. Despite the obvious pain, he continued to play until Josh Mahoney finally came on with about 12 minutes to go. What are his memories of that occasion and of the return to Stoke the following day? "Making the record was a nice distraction as we built up to the final, but, on the day itself, we knew we would win. We were the underdogs, but we felt relaxed and went out to enjoy the occasion. I felt relaxed and, as we walked up the tunnel and saw the mass of red and white of our supporters, we just got a great buzz. We had this kind of camaraderie which made us more determined to go out and win. As for the match itself, I was on the receiving end of a naughty tackle. I kind of rode it, but fell awkwardly on my shoulder. Whilst it was very painful, I didn't want to come off and didn't let on just how bad it really was. As for my part in the winning goal, it was really the result of hours on the training ground. Both John and I were ideally positioned as the ball came across from Terry. John headed it down to me and I volleyed it, as I had done on so many occasions before, toward the goal. Peter Bonetti managed to parry it out and the two wise old men, George and Peter, were there hoping to collect any rebound. As we all know, it was a fairy tale ending, as George slipped it into the net. We went up to the Royal Box to collect our tankards and all the feelings of the pain from my shoulder totally disappeared. It was just fabulous as we each received our awards and acknowledged the cheers of our fans. The return home was one of the best days of my life and is a day that will live with me for the rest of my life. I was totally gobsmacked by the enormity of the emotions that we experienced that weekend".

Back to the reality of league and cup football, as Stoke continued to press for more honours and another semi-final appearance against Arsenal. Looking back, Jimmy is magnanimous in his description of the Gunners, saying; "They proved they were a very good side and in reality, deserved to be 'double' winners".

Jimmy's career with Stoke came to an abrupt end in 1976, following the collapse of the roof of the Butler Street Stand. The club were under-insured and as such, were forced to sell their best players just to survive. It was a time that, as he looks back at his career in football. still brings back painful

Pic. E. Fuller

memories, because as he says; "I never wanted to leave Stoke at all. I had a meeting with the directors and was told of the position the club was in. I told them I didn't want to leave and had already told Tony this. But one of the directors turned to me and said: 'To be honest with you Jimmy, we think you're past it!' That made my mind up for me and I turned to Tony and said, 'I'm sorry boss. but I'll be signing for United tomorrow. It was all because of that pillock saying I was past it and I wanted to prove him wrong. Which, I think I did at United".

Jimmy proved his critics wrong by playing 122 games and scoring 36 times for the Red Devils, including two F.A. Cup final appearances. As he says: "That was a good record. We had a good midfield, who were able to score 15- 20 goals each, as well as having Stuart Pearson alongside me, who was a recognised goal-scorer. So I don't think I did too badly there, do you? In 1977, I had a dream come true, when I played in the F.A. Cup winning side, but, even then I would still have preferred it to have been with Stoke. Then, two seasons later, we got there again. Stoke were playing at home on the same night we played Liverpool in the semi-final replay. I scored with about 12 minutes left and have since been told that the score was announced at the Victoria Ground and I got such a cheer from the Boothen Enders. It made a great impression on me and made me realise just what I meant to them and what they meant to me".

Following a glittering career with Manchester United Jimmy left to play for Crewe Alex. This was, in a way, a move of opportunity for the fair-haired striker, as it was to allow him the chance to play in America, for Toronto Blizzard - a time which he recalls well. "Waddo was at Crewe and it was only for a couple of months, then I went to the States, but the standard of play was so bad, that even Crewe, who were at the bottom of the 4th division, would have beaten them. But saying that, it was an experience that I enjoyed".

Jimmy returned to these shores and signed for Port Vale. He didn't really want to because of the Stoke/Vale rivalry, but did so because of his connections with their directors, Don Ratcliffe and Jim Lloyd. It wasn't the best of times, as he recalls: "I didn't really get on with John McGrath. I think he thought I might be there to take over, so my time there, despite winning promotion, wasn't that enjoyable".

Following this, Jimmy moved into management, working alongside his brother Brian at Rochdale. He managed to keep them in the same division by avoiding relegation, but was let down badly by the directors of the club, who had promised him additional funding to strengthen the side, should they avoid the drop. This money was not forthcoming, so Jimmy was left with no alternative than to leave, having felt so let down.

He returned to the Potteries and to Vale Park, where he joined the coaching staff. However, this didn't really work out for Jimmy and he left the world of professional football. Following a stint as a footballing coach for Butlin's, Jimmy returned to Stoke-on-Trent, running his own business for many years. Today, he still works in the area and is an avid follower of his beloved Stoke City, attending as many matches as he can at the Britannia Stadium.

Looking back over a glittering career that included 5 England under-23 caps and representative caps for the Football League XI Jimmy cites: "The League Cup Final was my most memorable experience. I know I had been there before with Leeds, but this was something very special indeed. As for my favourite goal? That has to be the one which won the 'Goal of the Season' award from Central Television in 1974, for the goal I scored against my old club, Birmingham City at St. Andrews".

Jimmy can also be heard on B.B.C. Radio Stoke, where his expert analysis often enhances the match commentary. But, as he says: "It is hard to be objective when

I still love my team!" A feeling that is still a two-way affair, as the Stoke City fans still worship the name of '**Greenhoff**'.

Pic. E. Fuller

9

Pic. E. Fuller

John Ritchie

Born in Kettering on 12th July 1941, 'Reg' originally joined the Potters in 1962, for a fee of £2,500 from Kettering Town. 'Big' John had two spells at the Victoria Ground, spending three seasons with Sheffield Wednesday between 1966 and 1969, before 'coming home'. He made his League debut in 1963 against Cardiff City. John played in all 12 games during the League Cup run, scoring 4 goals in the process.

This chapter has been kindly supported in memory of Norman Peake.

Legend has it that Tony Waddington signed the man who would become Stoke's most prolific scorer, without even seeing him play. John, however, cannot corroborate this story, when he says: "That's how the story goes, but whether or not it is true, I don't really know. However, that's Tony for you, isn't it? He was always here and there signing players. You heard that he'd been some where and the next moment, he had signed someone like Peter Dobing or Dennis Viollet. But at £2,500, I wasn't really a major signing. He'd heard I could score a few goals, as I had been doing for Kettering Town in the Southern League - Bobby Wilde had spoken to him about me".

Stoke weren't the only club to have shown an interest in the young striker, as two other league teams, including Northampton Town, had approached him. Indeed, Dave Bowen, the Cobblers boss, was poised to sign John, but as he recalls, it didn't quite go to plan: "The Northampton manager made an approach for me, which, at the time, would have suited me down to the ground. They were my local club, but there was a problem as he told me he had to go into hospital for a heart operation. I told him I would prefer to wait until he had recovered, before committing myself. Then Tony came in for me one Thursday evening, during the time that he (Bowen) was in hospital, and made an offer which Kettering duly accepted and I made the move to Stoke. A move that, I think, was the best result for both Stoke City and myself".

John made a great start at Stoke, making 42 appearances and scoring 30 goals in his first full season with the club. This included a first team debut in the Welsh capital, at Ninian Park against Cardiff City. The following season, he gained a regular place and, alongside the only other player to have played for Stoke in two League Cup finals - Peter Dobing - played in the two-legged final against a Gordon Banks - inspired Leicester City. The 'Foxes' finally won 4-3 but, as John recalls, it could have been so different: "It was an amazing transition from the Southern League to the Central League, where I was lining up with players I had only seen on television and playing at places like Goodison Park, Old Trafford and Turf Moor, in front of crowds of 14,000 plus. This is more than the average gate at many of today's second division clubs. We finished 3rd in the Central League and scored over 100 goals between us in the process. I was lucky enough to play in the 1st team as well, having made my debut against Cardiff City. I played a total of 5 senior games that year. I suppose the most important game I played in was at Bolton, when I scored twice in the 4-3 thriller which sent them down instead of us. The following year, I played more and more 1st team games, including the two-legged League Cup Final against Leicester City. Today, Gordon (Banks) and I still talk about those two games. In particular I remember one save that he made, with only three minutes to play, which denied me from getting the equaliser. I hit the ball like a rocket from just inside the penalty area toward the top corner of the net. I turned to celebrate, convinced that I had scored, only to hear the roar of the crowd. Looking over my shoulder, I saw he had made an amazing save, punching the ball against the crossbar. Years later, when we trained together Gordon would remind me of that save when he

Pic. E. Fuller

would shout: 'you've got to do better than that Reggie, you know'. In my opinion, the man who beat us was simply the best the world has ever seen".

John's career took a dramatic change of direction in November 1966, as he left the Victoria Ground for pastures new at Hillsboro' with Sheffield Wednesday. However, as John explains, the move – which Tony Waddington later described as the 'biggest mistake that I ever made'- wasn't of his doing: "It was made to look as though it was my decision to go and that simply wasn't true. The club asked me to meet Alan Brown, the then Sheffield Wednesday manager, which, out of courtesy, I did. I explained to him that this is my club and I didn't want to go to Sheffield, as I loved playing for Stoke City. He replied by saying: 'he admired my spirit and stance of standing up for my principles, but could he speak to me for a little while?' However, after listening to him for a quarter of an hour or so, I told him that I hadn't changed my mind, as I still saw my future as lying at the Victoria Ground. So, excusing myself, I left the boardroom and went down to see Tony Waddington. He asked me whether or not I had signed for Wednesday. I told him that I hadn't and asked why – was I being forced to go? He answered, saying that I'd better go into his office and speak to the chairman. The chairman explained to me that Stoke were in dire straits and that the bank was threatening to foreclose their account and, as such, they wouldn't be able to pay the players' wages. So, in reality, they forced my hand and I joined Sheffield Wednesday. A similar thing happened in 1978, when the Butler Street Stand blew down and they forced Jimmy (Greenhoff) to go".

During his time at Hillsboro', John was selected to play for the Football League XI, against the League of Ireland at Dalymount Park in Dublin. He lined up alongside several of the England World Cup winning side and squad, including both fullbacks, George Cohen and Ray Wilson, whilst his striking partner was Jimmy Greaves. Recalling that he had scored two goals in the 7-2 victory, John says: "As we were coming off after the game, Jimmy Greaves turned to me and said 'you played well son, but even if you'd scored another goal for your hat-trick, he (Alf Ramsey) still wouldn't choose you, because he knows the side that he wants". John accepted this and, rather modestly, plays down his true footballing stature.

In 1969, Tony Waddington righted the mistake he made three years earlier, by re-signing the talented centre-forward for £20,000, but, as John remembers, his relationship with the club actually continued during his enforced exile in Sheffield; "Alan Brown was the nicest and most honest manager that I ever met. He was also truly concerned about his playing staff and he expressed this to me because as I used to travel up to Sheffield every day. He enquired whether or not it was having an effect on me because he would let me train with Stoke on a Friday if I wanted to. In the end, that is what I did and really felt the benefit in the long run. Then, I did indeed come back in 1969. We were on our annual summer holiday in Bournemouth, as I remember and we had gone down to the beach. Sometime mid-morning, one of the hotel waiters came running onto the beach and, tracking us down, told me that the hotel manager needed to speak to me immediately. I raced back to the hotel and found him with his hand over the receiver, whispering: 'its Tony Waddington, I think that he wants to re-sign you'. I told him not to joke about something like that and taking the 'phone, I enquired who was speaking. Tony confirmed his identity and after the usual pre-amble, asked if I would like to return to Stoke. Explaining that I was still on my holiday, I told him I would contact him upon my return and rung off. About 30 minutes after we had got back, the 'phone rang and Tony invited me down to talk to him. I said I would go down later in the day". He did so and 'the Leader' as the Boothen-Enders christened him, duly returned to his rightful position as Stoke City's centre forward and Tony Waddington had put the final two pieces in his jigsaw, as two weeks later, they signed Jimmy Greenhoff.

The new striking partnership proved to be an instant success, with John scoring 16 goals during the first season back at the Victoria Ground. They continued to play together and, like Denis and Alan in defence and George and Peter in midfield, John and Jimmy were a great double act. They both knew and worked to each other's strengths. This was particularly evident in the '71- 72 season. During the League Cup run, both strikers were ever present, scoring 7 goals between them – John getting 4 and Jimmy, the other 3. But what does he recall of that season? " Looking back at that period, I remember that we played in the previous seasons F.A. Cup semi-final. We were 2-0 up after 20 minutes and, by half-time, it really should have been all over, as we should have had another 3 goals. Jimmy broke through twice and should have made it 4-0. Then Josh hit a cracking shot, which Wilson just got to However, we all know the rest, don't we?"

"We seemed to go from strength to strength, having that great run in the League Cup the next year. Yes, I was ever present during that run, but what the majority of our fans didn't know, was that I played throughout the first part of the run with a broken toe. The doctor would come into the dressing room and give Frank Mountford a freezing spray to put on my foot. I literally couldn't feel anything, but, once the game was over and I got back into the warmth, the pain would return. However, it didn't seem to hold me back too much, as I managed to score 4 goals and, I think that I was unlucky not to have had two in the final itself. The first was in the replay against Oxford United at the Victoria Ground. Then I got two against Manchester United. The fourth, and most important goal was against

Pic. E. Fuller

West Ham United, in the 2nd leg of the semi-final. We were losing 2-1 and I managed to score just before half-time to level the scores. Unfortunately, that gets forgotten now because the thing that most people tend to remember - and talk about - was how Gordon's save kept us in the game. Like he says and I am in total agreement, while both of us played an important part in that particular game, it is a team sport and that is what is important. Every one who took part in the run deserves the praise, not just Gordon and myself. It's just that our parts in that match were the ones that are easily remembered. I should have had another in the semi-finals though, as I was going to take a penalty, should we get one. As everybody knows, we did indeed get a penalty in the 2nd replay at Old Trafford. Indeed it was me who earned it. It is the only time that I ever played for a penalty in my life! I didn't actually take a dive, but instead, seeing the position that the young defender McDowell was in, I manoeuvred myself into such a position that I knew he would hit me and knock me over. He did so and the ref. duly awarded the penalty. As I was getting up, ready to take the kick, Bernie had already

Pic. E. Fuller

grabbed the ball and placed it on the spot. The rest is history, as he managed to convert the rebound. I also got the ball in the net during the final itself, with quite a good header; however the referee blew and signalled that I was offside. Peter Houseman, who - a couple of years later – tragically died in a car accident, also managed to prevent me from getting onto the scoresheet - after I had beaten Bonetti with another header - as he cleared the ball off the line. I was lucky enough to have a part in our winning goal though. As the ball came across, I managed to head it back to Jimmy Greenhoff, in a move which Alan Brown had taught me at Sheffield. Nine times out of ten, Jim's volley would have hit the back of the net, but Peter Bonetti managed to palm it out. As we all know, George pounced and thumped it into the back of the net and, if I remember correctly, it was also the first time he got into the box that day!"

Like the other members of that victorious squad, John was amazed at the sheer volume - and feeling of emotion - of the crowd which greeted them on their return to the Potteries, as he says: "Tony told us in the hotel on the Sunday morning that the train would be stopping at Barlaston and we would be driven into Stoke on an open topped coach. I remember that it was very dark as we got onto the coach and all we could see was a continuous mass of illuminated red and white. It got more and more emotional as we got closer to Stoke. I remember looking at Alan and Denis, each with a tear in their eye, as we went through the Meir after we had made them carry the cup – it was absolutely fabulous! The sound just continued to get louder as we got closer to Stoke. It was wonderful and when we got about 50-yards away from the Town Hall entrance, the coach was forced to stop because of the sheer size of the crowd. So, we had to battle our way through on foot to the reception. I think the release of so much pent up emotion was due to the fact that the fans had had to wait for over 100 years to see their team bring home a trophy. But it was worth it, as all that physical emotion created such a euphoric moment. I realised then, and still think, that it was our fans who were the true winners that weekend".

Back to reality and a second F.A. Cup semi-final in as many seasons - once again where they were to meet Arsenal. "We got used to losing to them, didn't we? I must admit that they were a good side and were a little more disciplined than us, but, what certainly didn't help our cause, was the atrocious refereeing decisions which went against us at Goodison in the replay. The strange thing was, that the week afterwards, when we played Burnley at Turf Moor, we had the same ref. Before the match started, the door of the dressing room opened and he walked in to check our studs, Tony Waddington told him to get out, because one or two of us were a little hot-headed and still upset about his errors. However, he did come in, telling us that he still had to check our studs and to be fair to him he said: ' I'm holding my hand up, I did make a mistake last week'. We basically told him where to go! After that everything was okay and we just got on with the game. But, I bet he still feels awful about his mistake – and so he should!"

The following year saw the Potters mount their first ever challenge in Europe, when they were drawn to play Kaiserslauten in the EUFA Cup. John has good reason to recall it well, as he describes the two-legged affair; "We played the first leg at the Victoria Ground and won 3-1. I'd had a tussle throughout the game with a Yugoslavian, who played for them, as we knocked each other about a bit. This didn't stop me scoring though. So, by the time the 2nd leg came around, there was a bit of bad feeling between us. However, following the first leg, Tony dropped me, which seemed to be his normal knee-jerk reaction when things weren't going to plan. I wasn't selected for either of the following two games and, in reality, didn't expect to be going to Germany. He told me that he wanted me to travel with the team. I didn't really want to go just to sit on the bench and watch and if that had been the situation, I probably would have asked to leave the club, as I felt that I'd already played my part during the 1st leg. Tony told me that there were one or two injuries and I would be taking some part in the match. He named me as one of the sub's. Anyway, he decided to bring me on to replace Geoff Hurst, who wasn't making any great impression on the game. The substitution took place as we had just won a free-kick. I jogged on, from the bench behind the goal, toward the centre circle and, running past the Yugoslav that I 'd had that tussle with in the 1st leg, felt a sudden sharp pain in the kidney area. He'd thrown a punch at me as I went past, my arms raised in the automatic reaction of pain just as the referee turned around. All he saw was my raised arm as the Kaiserlauten player threw himself to the ground. He'd conned the ref. who promptly sent me off. So I just continued to jog off to the other end of the ground, where I met up with an uncomprehending Bluto, who hadn't seen the incident and couldn't understand what I was doing there beside him".

This was almost 'the straw that broke the camels back' for John, who was already disenchanted with the way that Tony Waddington kept using him as the scapegoat when things weren't going the Potters way. He was even contemplating the possibility of asking for a transfer. However, as that evening wore on and he was having a few drinks with Alan Bloor, the big defender managed to persuade John to stay.

The following season saw the Potters mount a serious challenge for the league title and John was an integral part of it. But, that participation came to an abrupt end, when Stoke travelled to Portman Road to play Ipswich Town. "It was the season in which we had more than our fair share of broken legs; added to that, was the board's determination not to spend any money on strengthening a greatly depleted side and that's what cost us the title! But, in my case, the break was so serious that I knew I would never play professional soccer again. It was the result of a really dirty tackle by Beattie. He caused what is known as a 'spiral fracture' and, if it hadn't have been for the skills of an amazing surgeon, I probably wouldn't have been able to walk properly again. The operation took five and a half hours and he had to put a metal bar in my leg and build a jigsaw of metal and bone around it. In reality, that tackle finished my playing career, but I was determined to rebuild the muscle in my leg and did so to the degree where I was able to think about the future. I managed a few matches with Stafford Rangers, before finally hanging my boots up for the last time".

John's future was already mapped out, as in 1970, he had had the foresight to open his own business, just a couple of hundred yards away from the Victoria Ground, in Lonsdale Street. Today, over thirty years later, it is still a thriving concern and he has been joined in the endeavour by his wife and family as they have just moved to larger premises in Stoke.

Finally, there are two questions to be asked of this modest, but truly great, centre-forward. The first is what was his favourite goal? Whilst the second is what is his fondest footballing memory? "As for the 'best' goal, well there have been so many. In the sense of importance, it must be the goal which kept us in the League Cup at West Ham. But to a striker, any goal is a good goal. However, I think the one that does stand in my mind, was the goal I got against Coventry City in front of the Boothen-End. They had been attacking and I'd gone back to help in defence. We managed to break out and raced down the pitch. The ball was pushed into the inside-left channel and I got it past the big centre half, (Blockley – I think). As the ball bounced, I flicked it back over him as he sped past me. Turning, I hit the ball on the volley from just outside the penalty area and it flew into the top of the net past their (immobile) 'keeper. From a technical point of view, I would say that has to be the best one I ever scored. My favourite memory doesn't actually revolve around the League Cup victory, which was important, but instead, it revolves around a game I took part in, in 1965 - Stanley Matthews testimonial game. It was in the middle of the season and I'd played around a dozen or so games and managed to score a few goals. Stan came up to me and said: 'I want you to come to the game tonight with the thought of playing'. I was amazed and told him that he must be joking - I'd not played very many games that season. He told me I would be on the bench, but would take part in the game at some stage. At half time, as they were leaving the pitch, with the Rest of the World side leading 3-1, Stan tapped me on the shoulder and told me I would be starting the second half. So, there was I, playing against the likes of Di Stefano, Puskas and the legendary Lev Yashin - it was just amazing. I had the pleasure of scoring against the great man, but not until I'd blazed the ball high over the crossbar in the second minute, as Yashin looked at me and said 'no problem son'. However, twenty minutes later, I scored! The ball flew into the top corner of the net. Just to have been a part of that night was truly amazing!"

Pic. E. Fuller

10

Pic. E. Fuller

Peter Dobing

Born on 1st December 1938 in Manchester, "Pierre" joined Stoke in 1963, having played for Blackburn Rovers and Manchester City, for a fee of £38,000. He made his debut against Tottenham Hotspur in 1963. Skippering Stoke, Pierre played in 10 of the 12 games during the cup run and scored 3 goals during that time. He will be forever remembered as the man who led Stoke to their first ever trophy.

This chapter has been kindly supported on behalf of Christine Glenn.

Peter turned his back on a very promising academic career at Nantwich Grammar School to join the groundstaff at Blackburn Rovers. Why choose Blackburn? "At the time I had gained seven G.C.E. 'O' levels and was in the sixth form doing my 'A' levels when both Manchester United and Blackburn Rovers offered me terms. I remember", Peter continues, "that the headmaster, Mr. Morris, tried his hardest to get me to finish my education before signing for one or the other club. However, I decided to join Blackburn. Why Blackburn and not United? Well, in all honesty, I looked at both sides and saw that the Rovers 1st team had an older element with players such as; Tommy Briggs, Eddie Quigley and Eddie Crossan and others who were all in their 30s. Whereas, at Old Trafford, it was the time of the 'Busby Babes' with Bobby Charlton, Duncan Edwards, Tommy Taylor etc. All these youngsters were coming up, so on balance I thought I would stand a better (and quicker) chance of getting into Blackburn's 1st team than at Manchester. Looking back at my decision, I think that I probably wouldn't be talking to you today as I would more than likely have been with the United team on the 'plane that crashed in Munich, had I chosen them over Blackburn. As it was, I was actually in the barracks having been called-up that day to do my National Service. I can't help thinking there but for the hand of fate went I. However, the 'plane crash apart, I think that I made the right choice because Johnny Carey (the Blackburn manager) put me in the 1st team by the time I was seventeen and a half".

Peter, a more than useful inside forward, soon established himself in the Blackburn side and was an integral part of their progression to the 1959-60 F.A. Cup Final, where they met Wolverhampton Wanderers. Blackburn lost 3-0 but despite the loss, does Peter have fond memories of the day? "It was in the days before substitutes and our full-back David Whelan (he laughs and describes him as a 'pauper' nowadays – as he is the owner of JJB Sports and is worth an estimated 1.3 billion) broke his leg in the first 10 minutes of the game, so we were down to ten men and on a pitch that size we really stood no chance at all. So it proved as they beat us 3-0. But as for actual memories of the game I don't really have any. Instead, I suppose I have feelings about the place instead, I never enjoyed playing there, it was too big! By that, I mean that the pitch was too far away from the crowd so we didn't feel the atmosphere. As I recall, there were other grounds like that – Chelsea's Stamford Bridge and Bristol Rovers Eastville come to mind – stadiums that didn't have any atmosphere when we played there. However, back to that day, the only other thing I can recall was the dressing-room at half-time and Dave's screams of agony as the doctors tried to set his leg".

Away from the world of football, Peter showed that he was something of an all-rounder, by playing cricket for Lancashire. "I was on the groundstaff at Old Trafford and played several 2nd team fixtures against Cheshire and the like, before getting called-up as 12th man for the 'Roses' game at Headingley. I actually got onto the pitch as Geoff Pullar – the opening batsman injured himself and I had to field. I recall that

Pic. E. Fuller

I felt a bit out of place being on the same cricket pitch as players such as Brian Statham, however at the lunch interval the 'great' Fred Truman took me under his wing as we dined together".

When it came to the crunch, Peter decided that he would probably be a better footballer than cricketer so he chose that as his profession. While he was at Blackburn he won several under 23 caps and was also chosen for the full squad on two occasions. As he recalls; "I was on the verge of winning a full cap having been called up as a reserve for the game in Luxembourg, which we won 9-0 (I think). I was called-up as a reserve for the next game, which was at Wembley, against Spain. After the game we all went to the official reception and unbeknownst to me the Blackburn chairman gatecrashed the evening with the girl that I was seeing at that time. The stiff upper-lipped selectors didn't see the funny side of that and I was never selected again".

After a couple of years at Ewood Park Peter thought that a change of scene would further his career: "It was at the time of George Eastham's lawsuit against Newcastle United and the abolishment of the maximum wage. Well, the then Fulham chairman Tommy Trinder had been quoted by the press as wanting to pay Johnny Haynes £100 a week, whilst the maximum at Blackburn was only £20. The directors made us a collective offer which would see us having a rise of the princely sum of £5 to £25 per week. I thought that while Haynes was a very good player there was no way that that he was worth four times more than me, so I rejected the offer and asked for a move. Newcastle United saw me as the natural replacement for George Eastham who had just joined Arsenal. So I went up to St. James' Park to train with them for a week and met the Magpies manager Charlie Mitten and Jimmy Schoular. They asked what I wanted as a signing-on fee. I asked for £3000 but Charlie Mitten only offered me £1000. As I didn't like the atmosphere I declined their offer and, having packed my boots and kit, I walked out. However, I bumped into Newcastle's chairman who said to me ' I don't know how you young lads can afford to turn down £3000', so it appears that Charlie was going to pocket the rest. So in all honesty, I'm glad I didn't go to the North East".

Manchester City, the club that Peter had supported as a boy, also approached Blackburn with the aim of gaining the young inside-forward's signature. It was too good an opportunity to miss, so Peter duly became a City player. In retrospect was it such a good move for the talented Dobing? "Initially I saw it as a fabulous opportunity for me as I was being given the chance to play for the club that I had supported as a child, coming from Manchester as I do. It was similar to the situation that I faced when I originally signed for Blackburn as City were in a stage of flux as they were replacing many of their ageing stars – players such as Dave Ewing and the legendary Bert Trautmann. Looking back I think that it wasn't the best move that I could have made as I rather let my heart rule my head when it came to the choice of a new club. At that time Manchester City were also very similar to the Stoke City side as their performances were inconsistent. They would play well against the stronger sides and then lose to teams that they should really have beaten with ease. This inconsistency led to us (Man. City) being relegated at the end of the 1962-63 season whilst Stoke City were going in the other direction as they had just won the 2nd division title".

Tony Waddington, in his attempt to strengthen the squad that had just won promotion, approached Manchester City asking whether Peter was available. It became evident that Peter was surplus to requirement at Maine Road. However, he recalls Stoke was not the only club to enquire about him, when he says: "Arsenal made an offer for me and I could very well have joined George Eastham at Highbury, instead of him joining me several seasons later here at Stoke. At the time I didn't fancy living in London and the Arsenal ground has never been one of my favourites, so I rejected the move. However, Waddo and Harry Ware (the then chief scout at the Victoria Ground) who was a good friend of my father contacted me through my dad – and I became a Stoke City player. Looking back at the time I spent at Stoke I can honestly say that it was the most enjoyable period of my professional career. Apart from the fact that the move kept me in the 1st division it also gave me the opportunity to play alongside such legendary players as Stan Matthews, Jackie Mudie and Dennis Viollet".

As with both Manchester City and Blackburn, Waddo was rebuilding the Stoke side that had won promotion as many of the players were coming to the end of their careers. He was doing this by cleverly blending a mix of experience with young local talent. Indeed, one of the 'older' players to join Stoke in the next couple of seasons was George Eastham, with whom Peter was to create an outstanding midfield partnership which, but for the hand of fate, may have already have existed at Highbury. However, it wasn't until 1966 that the duo finally came together.

Pierre (as Dennis Viollet nicknamed Peter) and Skippy (as George became known to his team-mates), aided and abetted over the next few years by a supporting cast of players such as Gerry Bridgewood, Alan Philpott et al, brought a new dimension to the style in which the Potters performed. As Peter, when describing this period, pays tribute to his midfield partner, says: "Yes it was a great thrill to be able to play alongside George and to build such an understanding between us that must have appeared to have been almost telepathic. He and I were on the same wavelength, which made it a lot easier when we were on the pitch. I knew where he would be and vice-versa, this came with the experience of playing and training together week in and week out. It was most enjoyable as he made it so easy for me and (hopefully) I made it easier for him too".

Amongst the earlier highlights of his time at Stoke was the summer tournament in the U.S.A. where Stoke 'guested' in the new North American Soccer League as the Cleveland Stokers. It was an experiment to introduce football to the Americans, with Clubs from all over the world taking part. Sunderland, Wolves and the Potters were joined by Glentoran, Celtic and several top South American clubs – all playing under new names. Peter recalls one incident which highlighted the talent on show in the States when he recalls; "We were invited to represent Cleveland (Ohio) and played at the Cleveland Indians baseball stadium. The name came from the Indians owner Vernon Stoker, he was a hotelier with hotels all across the States. He was trying to keep sport alive in Cleveland, as the average Indians attendance (in that massive stadium) being between 2 and 3000. It was a great experience but one incident on the night before our 'away' game against Sunderland stands out in my mind. At that time they had the great 'Slim' Jim Baxter playing for them. Anyway, on the night before the game he was in the bar knocking quite a few pints back – after which he made an astonishing verbal attack on the directors of Sunderland claiming that they were most unprofessional. He played against us the following day and completely wiped the floor with us".

"On another occasion we played against one of the South American sides and they kicked lumps out of us. After one of them kicked me I'm afraid I lost my temper and thumped him. He fell to the floor as though he had been pole-axed. That set off a chain reaction with every member of their squad rushing into the centre-circle and starting a mass punch-up. Their 'keeper ran half the length of the pitch to kick Maurice Setters on the backside. He then ran off toward the dressing rooms with Maurice in hot pursuit. The referee finally restored the peace and promptly sent Josh Mahoney off. John's only contribution to the melee had been to jump on my back as he tried to stop me throwing any more punches".

Back to England and the bread and butter scene of league and cup football and, as Peter said earlier, Stoke continued to play attractive but inconsistent football. One week they would win by a convincing margin and the next they would be beaten against a side that had no right of winning. One such victory which demonstrates this was the 3-2 win over Leeds United, a game in which Peter scored a hat-trick. Does he remember that game? "I remember that it was a midweek game and for some reason I always played better under floodlights. It was at a time when Leeds had won a 'hell' of a lot of games and would have created a new record had they won the game against us. We were two goals up and they equalised, which made the last quarter of the game very exciting indeed! I then got the third goal but they literally threw everything at us. Our goal faced an amazing onslaught but we kept every shot out and won. If I remember correctly it was also the night that saved us from relegation that season as well, so it was a job well done".

By 1969 Waddo had finished rebuilding his side and Stoke, instead of being the annual underdogs, were about to mount a real challenge for some trophies. They reached the F.A.Cup semi-final only to be beaten after a replay by Arsenal. Peter, however, missed both games as he had broken his leg earlier in the season. He recalls: "I was out for twelve months but was at both games to add my support to the lads. I thought that we deserved to win at Hillsborough but they were the better side in the replay. I think that the referee got it wrong but that still happens today, so until we are in the position to utilise modern technology – as they do in cricket or rugby league we will just have to put up with refereeing errors – as we did then".

Peter, a veteran of Stoke's previous League Cup final – when they lost 4-3 to Leicester City over a two-legged game. "I remember that we had the majority of the play in the second game at Filbert Street and should have beaten them. There was one attack when the ball came to me. I was only about three yards out with an empty open goal in front of me. I hit the ball, only to see Banksie appear from

129

nowhere to make another exceptional save. In reality that second match was a game of Banksie against us. So in later years I was rather glad that he signed for Stoke". Peter played an important part in the cup run itself, especially against West Ham where in the second replay at Old Trafford he scored the 2nd goal, he remembers it well saying; "After Hillsborough, where I nearly cost us the game with a mis-placed back-pass that forced Gordon, once again, to make an amazing save that kept us in the competition. We went to Old Trafford and played well despite the awful conditions. My goal came as we were mounting another attack. This time through George Eastham. He slipped the ball across the edge of the penalty area to me and I just turned and hit it inside the post. Funnily enough I can still remember the droplets of water that cascaded down as the ball hit the back of the net. Then T.C. scored what proved to be the winner and we were through to a Wembley final at last".

By the time of the final itself, Peter was carrying an injury and there was some doubt about whether or not he would play. "However, on the day before the final I had a little run out and was declared fit, so I played. The game itself went by so quickly that I cannot really recall that much about it. I can't even remember climbing the steps and receiving the trophy or the lap of honour afterwards, it was all just a blur. But what I do remember was the day after. We didn't know what to expect when we returned but there were so many people lining The streets as we were driven from Barlaston to Stoke that it was unbelievable. Being a shy person it was a bit embarrassing but fantastic at the same time".

Back to the normality and reality of league and cup football as Stoke battled through to a second successive F.A.Cup semi-final, once again against losing in a controversial manner to Arsenal. Peter recalls it well, especially after he had made the promise "to bring back the F.A. Cup in May – to add it to this one" as he stood on the balcony at the Kings Hall showing the League Cup off to the assembled multitude, as he says: "After the match I remonstrated with the referee and the linesman about both goals. The penalty

Pic. E. Fuller

130

shouldn't have been given, as I never touched little Geordie Armstrong, even though he fell like a sack of potatoes. As for the second goal! Charlie George was so far offside that he could have been having a Bovril at the back of the terraces behind our goal. However, to the credit of the linesman he did own up to me that he had made a glaring error of judgement".

Peter's career in football came to an end soon after the Wembley victory as a persistent back injury steadily worsened and was having a serious effect upon his mobility on the pitch, so as a 33 year old he was forced to call it a day. Denied a testimonial game by Stoke 'because we could not afford to stage such a game' Peter turned to the pottery industry to earn a living and for the next two decades ran his own business in the city. Today, having retired, he lives on the outskirts of Stafford with his family and whilst he doesn't visit the Britannia Stadium frequently he does keep in touch with many of his old playing colleagues. Looking back he cites his time at Stoke "as being the best and most enjoyable years of my career, not only did I enjoy playing but the people of the area treated me so well. Of course the League Cup win was the major highlight but so was playing with the 'greats' such as Banksie, Stan, Jimmy McIlroy and Dennis Viollet. Great memories that nobody can take away".

Pic. E. Fuller

11

Pic. E. Fuller

George Eastham O.B.E.

Born in Blackpool on 23rd September 1936, "Skippy" joined Stoke in 1966, for a fee of £50,000 from Arsenal. The former Ards and Newcastle United player, who was a member of the 1966 World Cup Winning squad, returned to Stoke from South Africa to play a significant part in the League Cup campaign. He played in 6 games, was substitute in three more and had the distinction of scoring the goal that secured a major trophy for Stoke for the first time in 108 years.

This chapter has been kindly supported on behalf of John Davey.

As this chapter begins we will set you, the reader, two questions. Firstly, what does George Eastham have in common with the former Hibs. Manchester United and Stoke striker David Herd? The second question is; what does George have in common with the former Nottingham Forest, Liverpool and Manchester City star and now Burton Albion boss Nigel Clough? The answers can be found at the end of this chapter.

Pic. E. Fuller

Born in Blackpool, George's professional career commenced in 1952, with the Irish club Newton Ards. He made his debut, in the reserves, "as a skinny little lad" – his own words, playing on the left wing alongside his father George Eastham snr. who was the player-manager and was playing at inside-left. George recalls that; "I felt very vulnerable out on the left flank, playing against what appeared to be a giant of a fullback. However, after a very heavy first tackle which nearly landed me in the crowd my father, who was keeping a protective eye on me, had a word – basically telling him that if he did that again it would be him rather than me who would end up in the crowd. As I recall we won 5-3 and I must have made such an impression upon the manager (smiles) that I managed to retain my place for the rest of the season".

George graduated to the Ards 1st team and won the first of his representative honours by being selected to play for the Football League of Ireland against the Republic of Ireland's League side. "I was selected again for the Irish League side to play against the English Football League in a game that we (Ireland) won 5-2. Shortly after that, I was transferred to Newcastle United". Reminiscing about his career, George suggested that; "I am probably unique in the fact that I played for the Irish League against England and later for the English Football League XI against their Irish counterparts whilst ending up on the winning side on both occasions, beating the Irish League 12-1 in 1966, just after we had won the World Cup".

George joined Newcastle in 1956 after being signed by Stan Seymour. As he recalls; "It was a time of transition in the north-east, the old guard who had appeared in the cup finals were being replaced by a new, younger, crop of players. We played some very exciting football, often scoring 4 or 5 goals a match. However, we had rather a leaky defence which more often than not would concede 5 or 6 in reply, thereby losing by the odd goal on many occasions". His stay with the Magpies lasted for 4 years and whilst, on the whole, it was an enjoyable experience as he gained several under 23 caps, his relationship with the club began to sour. This was in the days of the 'maximum wage'. As George remembers; "I was earning £20 per week and felt that I needed some extra so I approached the club to ask if they would object to me getting a small afternoon job. After due consideration, a relatively new board member offered me a job that involved visiting several local pubs and meeting the clientele for something like £5 per week. I couldn't really see myself doing that so I declined".

Pic. E. Fuller

Given the chance to work in London, George moved to work for a friend of his father. Newcastle, however, were dead set against this and quickly informed him that they had the right to retain his F.I.F.A. registration and as such he would never be allowed to ply his trade with any other football club. This led to the famous High Court case in front of Lord Chief Justice Wilberforce (the grandson of William Wilberforce - the abolitionist), who ruled in George's favour judging that Newcastle's hold on his contract was tantamount to slavery itself and as such he should be released from it.

Several months later Newcastle accepted an offer of £47,500 from the Arsenal boss George Swindin and he left the north-east for the hallowed halls of Arsenal's Highbury Stadium. Unfortunately for George, Mr. Swindin was replaced soon after that by Billy Wright, who had just retired from a playing career in which he gained a then record 105 international caps. Recalling this managerial upheaval, George says that; "Things altered after the arrival of Billy Wright, we had our ups and downs, but there was an undercurrent of support for me at the club at all levels from the boardroom through to the fans, so I felt that my future was relatively secure". Billy left, as he failed to bring any real success to the mighty Arsenal, and was replaced by Bertie Mee. The former club physiotherapist felt threatened by the powerbase that George had at Highbury and he transfer-listed George just after the successful World Cup win in 1966. Looking back George holds no hard feelings when he says; "Who am I to say that he (Bertie Mee) was wrong to let me go, after all despite the fact that he hadn't played at the top level, he obviously knew what he was doing as the Gunners went from strength to strength during his time in charge at Highbury".

So in August 1966, Tony Waddington offered Arsenal £50,000 for George, an offer which Mee felt he couldn't reject and Skippy duly signed for the Potters. As George says; "I entered the best, and happiest, phase of my footballing career. Stoke were in a state of flux as Tony Waddington was attempting to rebuild his side from the 2nd division championship winning team of 1963. Gone were players such as the legendary Stanley Matthews and Jackie Mudie and coming in were players such as Peter Dobing and myself. He had kept several of the younger players such as 'Alfie' Skeels and 'Tagger' Allen. Waddo had tried a variety of short-term replacements but was now planning for the future. In reality I think that the rebuilding started in 1966 and was finally completed in 1969 when he signed 'Reg' and Jimmy".

However, there would still be casualties of the rebuilding and John Farmer was to be one as Waddo approached George to ask his advice about the chance of obtaining the signature of a vital cog to the ideal team, George recalls the chat; " 'George,' he said, 'I can get Banksie for £50,000, do you think I should go for him.' I replied, that you must snatch him up before anyone else gets wind of him being available. So I spoke to Gordon and let him know about the club, after all we were England room-mates and the best of friends, so he joined us".

George went on to form an almost telepathic partnership with Peter Dobing and either Mike Bernard or John Mahoney in the supporting role. During the following few seasons the fans were treated to many magical moments as he and Pierre would tantalise the opposition with their artistic footwork. One such highlight was the game against Leeds United which the Potters won 3-2, rather against all the popular opinion of the day.

By the semi-final years (1970-72) George was planning for his future. Indeed, he began to combine the future with the present by playing for the Potters before jetting out to the warmer climate of South Africa, to become the player-manager of Hellenic. This was with the proviso that he would return to play for Stoke should they get to the F.A.Cup Final. However, as we all know now this didn't happen, so he completed the season in South Africa with a flourish. Not only did Hellenic do extremely well but George himself won a hatfull of awards including the 'Coca-Cola kid'. He returned to Stoke the following season, leaving his father George Eastham snr. in charge at Hellenic, in time for the league cup match against Manchester United at Old Trafford where, after getting special permission, Waddo named him as substitute. He was on the bench for all three games against United, coming on in both the replay and second replay, before reclaiming his number 11 shirt for the quarter-finals at Bristol through to the final itself. What, then, does he remember of the run? "To win against United, albeit at the third attempt, was something special – especially when you consider that they had players of the calibre of Best, Law and Bobby Charlton playing for them. Into the quarter-finals and we played down at Bristol Rovers but in reality the game as a spectacle was over after 20 minutes, as we were 2 goals up by then. The semi-finals against West Ham United were an epic in themselves, looking back I think that all four games created a tie that would have been worthy of the final itself. It was unbelievable, losing up here and going into the lions den, so to speak, and winning. And of course there was Gordon's fabulous penalty save, what more could you want. Then we went to Hillsboro', where really it was too cold to perform at our best, but both teams did try even though it did finish goal-less. Finally, there was the game at Old Trafford where Peter scored the winner. The emotion in the dressing room after was brilliant". Then came the final itself which George, who is a modest and retiring man, spoke very little of. However, when pressed, he did describe his memories of that great day, saying; "I remember John Marsh scrambling about on all fours looking for his contact lens, which had been dislodged and Terry's headed goal that proved Dave Sexton wrong, he could head the ball! " But what about the goal itself, what did he (George) remember of that moment? "Terry crossed the ball and 'big', John headed it down to Jimmy Greenhoff. Jimmy hit it goalward but Bonetti parried the ball out and it bounced nicely between me and Peter (Dobing). I remember screaming at him to 'get the hell out of the way' as it was at my speciality range of two yards and I just hit it into the net".

Was that the highlight of his career? Looking back George mused that; "I have been lucky, there have been so many highlights, like winning my first cap. South Africa was a highlight. There were two games for Arsenal, when we played our North London neighbours Tottenham drawing each time 4-4, both were games of splendour. Of course the League Cup Final was a highlight but there was also a match in Cape Town – a derby between us (Hellenic) and Cape Town in front of a crowd of 44,000 people, played in a ground which should have held only 26,000, now that had an electrical feel about it, it ended 2-2. I was also very lucky to play in stadiums such as the Maracana against the magical Brazilians. So, I reckon that I have been very lucky. These are memories which I will never forget".

Following the League Cup victory, George continued with the club until a cartilage injury curtailed his playing career. However, after a series of bad results Waddo left and George took over as manager. But as he says; "It did become a little awkward as I was suddenly in charge of players who the day before had been my team-mates. It took a bit of time to adjust. Alan A'Court and I wanted to buy O'Callaghan but the board wouldn't give us the money. (He later joined Stoke after Alan Durban took over). After this I began to feel disillusioned and soon left the club".

George returned to South Africa where he started his own sports goods business. A business which he ran successfully until he retired about four years ago. Today he still lives in South Africa, however with family still in Stoke on Trent he does visit the area occasionally. Indeed it was during his last visit (in 2001) for his son's wedding that he spoke to me about his life and times. Oh yes, and the answer to the two questions that were set at the beginning of this section is as follows:- George and David Herd both played professional football in the same side as their respective fathers. 2) George and Nigel Clough both followed their fathers footsteps and gained full England caps.

Pic. E. Fuller

12

Pic. E. Fuller

John Mahoney

Born in Cardiff on 20th September 1946, "Josh" joined Stoke from Crewe Alexandra for £10,500 in 1967, having previously played for Ashton United. He made his 1st team debut against Sunderland during the same season. He played in 4 games during the League Cup run and was on the subs. bench for another 6 matches including the final itself.

This chapter has been kindly supported by Alec and Jo Bohannan.

The first thing that is noticeable when meeting John Mahoney today, is that his accent has altered from the time he played at Stoke. Gone is the hard Mancunian tone and it has been replaced by the lilting sound of his native Wales. Looking back at his early days John remembers that; "My family moved from Cardiff, where I was born, to Manchester when I was only 8-years old because my father – Joseph – had signed to play Rugby League for Oldham".

Pic. E. Fuller

As a schoolboy the young John soon showed signs of becoming an excellent footballer. He joined Ashton United and played in the local league. However, he was soon gaining a reputation and was attracting the attention of the Crewe manager Ernie Tagg. Josh remembers that Ernie offered him a contract with Crewe; "I signed for the Alex part of the way through the season. I remember that we had several tough games and I was given an early chance to prove myself. But, it didn't quite go to plan as I received a thigh strain which hampered my game". John had impressed so much that he was offered terms for the following season, as he recalls; "There was I, a teenager in the early '60s getting a cheque every two weeks for £22, I thought I was really well off". The following season John became a regular for the Gresty Road side and was soon attracting the attention of the Welsh national manager. He says; "I remember when I got my first under 23 cap, the supporters club and the junior supporters were fantastic – they sent me so many good luck cards and messages. That I really felt very humble. What I didn't know was that Bill Shankly of Liverpool was interested in me and had been at the game to watch me. I remember that the game was abandoned eight minutes before time because of a blizzard and that several of the Irish lads had collapsed, suffering from the cold. However, I must have interested Mr. Shankly as I noticed that he was deep in conversation with my father on the flight back to England but at that time nothing came of it".

"Returning to the Alex, I remember that I even ended up in goal for one game. We were playing Lincoln City and Willie May, who as well as being our 1st team 'keeper was also my landlord, damaged his finger and had to go off. I volunteered to go between the posts and managed to keep a clean sheet which helped to get us a draw. After that I once again strained my hamstring and needed attention. Liverpool rekindled their interest in me by contacting Crewe and offering their physio's services to me". Tony Waddington also approached

Crewe with the intention of signing John at the same time as 'Shanks' made a bid. This gave Josh the choice of the two 1st division clubs. After some consideration the young Welshman decided that Stoke would be the better option for him and he duly signed for the Potters the day after they had obtained the services of a young flame-haired Irishman named Terry Conroy. As Josh recalls; "We signed together and have remained best friends ever since. Terry is godfather to one of my three daughters and likewise I am the same to one of his girls".

John managed to get a few 1st team matches under his belt after signing for the club. His greatest memory in those early days was that he got the chance to play alongside one of his boyhood heroes – Dennis Viollet, as he says; "I was a big Manchester United fan as a boy, so you can imagine how I felt coming off after my first game as Dennis came over to me to shake my hand and say well done!" Between 1967 and the '70-71 season John was in and out of the 1st team never really making one of the midfield slots his own. This was down to the fact that he collected a series of injuries including a cartilage problem that required surgery. However, his talents did shine through and he entered the international arena to make his full debut for Wales against England, as John himself describes; "My first full cap was against England. I wasn't in the original squad but due to injuries to several key members of the team Manager Dave Bowen gave me a late call-up into the squad. England had ten of their World Cup Winning side out against Wales that day and I can remember the way that Gordon (Banks) came up to me after the game to congratulate me on my first cap. My second cap came soon after as Wales were due to play East Germany in Dresden. I remember that we (Stoke) had a midweek match against Newcastle United. Both Ollie Burton, Wyn Davies and myself were allowed to join the rest of the squad after our league game. We arrived in Berlin and walked through Checkpoint Charlie into the East feeling a bit like Michael Caine as Harry Palmer, where an official car was waiting for us. I remember that we lost 2-1 going down to a last minute goal".

By the 1970-71 season Waddo had totally rebuilt the side and they started to challenge the top clubs for trophies. Indeed, they got to the F.A.Cup semi-final that season, only to be beaten by Arsenal and some dubious refereeing decisions. As the game at Hillsborough entered the last two minutes, the Potters were leading 2-1 and seemed destined to break their 107-year hoodoo by reaching a Wembley cup final for the first time. However, it was not to be as Arsenal mounted one last attack. To this day everybody, bar the three officials, is adamant that Gordon Banks was fouled and that Stoke should have been awarded a free kick. Neither Pat Partridge or either of his two linesmen saw the infringement and Arsenal were awarded a corner. The ball came over and Frank McLintock headed it toward the goal. John takes up the story; "Because I was one of the shorter players, I was covering the back post as usual. Frank McLintock got a header in that flew to my right, just inside the post. Really I had no other choice but to dive and punch it away. Looking back, I think that I thought well we've got Banksie so there will always be the chance that he'll save it. I know that nobody blames me but in some ways I will feel guilty about it". Storey kept his nerve and coolly slotted the ball past Banks to equalise and force a replay at Villa Park. "In this game you don't often get a second chance and that's how it panned out, as they beat us in the replay and went on to win the double. So it wasn't to be that year anyway".

Looking back at the League Cup Winning season, John thinks; "The experience of losing in such a way to Arsenal was not as negative an ordeal as many thought but, rather the opposite. It made us more determined not to repeat it again the following season". So it proved as the team once again gelled in cup competition, this time though it was in the League Cup. John was an integral part of the squad as he played in 4 games and was on the subs. bench for a further 4 matches including the final itself. What then does John remember of that cup run and did he have any special memories of the final itself? "I especially remember the games against my old favourites Manchester United. We deserved the draw up there at Old Trafford and should really have won. I had a couple of chances, which went begging. The first was scrambled away by Alex Stepney, while the second went off a defender for a corner. The second match was the draw at home, with the third match also being at the Victoria Ground. It was the best of the three as it had everything, including the winning goal from 'Reg' (John Ritchie) after T.C. and I worked the ball along the right wing. Then there was the semi-final, which was a saga in its own right, wasn't it? But I think that Ron Greenwood made a serious error, when their 'keeper was injured and Bobby Moore went in goal. He wasn't the fastest player in the world but he could read the game like a book and that was what they needed. However, they chose to do it that way and they certainly paid the price. But (laughingly) what do I remember is getting absolutely drowned as I sat on the bench waiting for my chance to get on the pitch".

Then, as John remembers, came the final itself with all the build up that surrounded it and the actual game and then the amazing celebrations afterwards, saying; "Terry and I went to London on the Monday to make an appearance on the Noel Edmonds show on Radio One. I remember that after the interview he asked us if we could get him a ticket for the final. The rest of the lads came down the following day and we met up at the Croydon hotel that became our hideaway for the next few days. We didn't feel the pressure, being away from it all and with many of the pundits seeing us as being the underdogs to boot, that really lifted the pressure off our shoulders. Waddo named the team later on during the week. I had mixed feelings when I found out that I was to be on the bench once again. I was happy to be involved with the final itself but obviously would have preferred to have been in the starting line-up".

"I don't remember much about the final itself, apart from the fact that Jimmy (Greenhoff) had been struggling for the majority of the game, so I was getting myself mentally prepared to come on at any time. But, Waddo left him on for as long as possible because it would have meant that we would have to alter the shape of the team and that would have posed less of a problem for Chelsea to contend with. However I did finally get on the pitch for the last five minutes or so. But I didn't really have enough time to make any real contribution to the game as the final whistle went soon after and we had won".

"I don't really remember the presentation but the lap of honour was indeed something special. I had played at Wembley for Wales on several occasions before but being there with Stoke and seeing the reaction of our fans was a very special moment that I will never ever forget. I will also remember the welcome we got the following day as we were driven through Stoke from Barlaston to the Kings Hall. It was fantastic and I can relate more to that than the games themselves because of the relationship that we (the players) had with you (the fans)".

After that, John suffered from a cartilage injury, which prevented him from playing in the replay of the F.A. Cup semi-final. It also kept him out for the rest of that season but he would return refreshed for the next year. "I was happy with life at the Victoria Ground and wanted to stay with Stoke. So I stayed, until the 1977-78 season, which was when things started to change. We lost the Butler Street Stand during a gale and as the club didn't have the right form of insurance they had to start economising. Waddo left and so did several key players including Jimmy Greenhoff who went to Manchester United and Pej. who went to Everton. The atmosphere within the club also changed and I began to feel that I might benefit by having a change myself. I could see that players like 'Shilts' (Peter Shilton) wouldn't look forward to playing clubs like Mansfield, whereas Middlesboro', who had made an offer for me, were playing Liverpool in the opening game of the season. So I decided to sign for John Neill at 'Boro. To me it really was the end of an era".

"Middlesboro' were reasonably successful, we got to the quarterfinals of the F.A. Cup in each of the two seasons that I was there. We played Orient in the first year and having drawn at home we travelled to London for the replay. It wasn't to be as we lost 2-1 and I suffered a broken leg, after Tony Grealish made a late tackle on me. So I missed the rest of the season. My second, and final season, at Ayrsome Park was less than memorable and I found myself moving to South Wales as I signed for the new Swansea boss (and my cousin) John Toshack. 'Tosh' made it sound like an adventure as I would be moving 'home' and would be playing alongside my international team-mates. Players such as (the late great) Robbie James, who later went to Stoke, Dai Davies, Alan Curtis and of course 'Tosh' himself who was the player-manager. After two seasons in division two we won promotion to the top flight".

Swansea, however, due to a certain amount of mis-management started to struggle both on and off the pitch. Josh finally departed, after another broken leg, to become the manager of Bangor City. Despite a lack of investment he was reasonably successful, steering them to the final of the Welsh F.A. Cup where they lost to Shrewsbury Town. However, because Shrewsbury is an English club they weren't allowed to represent Wales in the Cup Winners Cup so, by default, Bangor went on to contest that trophy. The highlight of the competition for John was the 2nd leg of the 2nd round tie against the mighty Athletico Madrid. As he recalls; "Despite losing 1-0 it was a moral triumph for us as we had been written off before the match even kicked off. The pundits had all claimed that the Spanish giants would hammer us into the ground. We proved that night that we could play at that level". As at Swansea, it was the off-field antics of certain individuals which caused financial problems for Bangor. This forced John's hand; he had had enough and rightly walked away from the club.

Following his experiences at Bangor, John was somewhat reticent about returning to the game he loved. However, Newport County approached him and so it was to be he returned to football. Once again though it was a case of 'out of the frying pan and into the fire' as there were serious financial problems within that club as well and it folded halfway through the season. Once again John found himself outside the game but there was another offer in the wind. Bangor City contacted him and asked if he would consider going back there. At the same time Carmarthen Town also contacted him and with two clubs to choose from he decided that it would be better to start afresh and duly joined Carmarthen. Commuting however took its toll and after two years he finally succumbed to the onset of osteo-arthritis and semi-retired from the game. Since then he has "helped out" at Conwy and Holywell on the coaching staff.

On the international front, Josh gained 51 full caps for Wales. He recalls the occasion of his 50th cap against Yugoslavia, saying: "We won with Robbie James and Rushie both getting on the scoresheet. But the funny thing that sticks in my mind happened as we returned to the airport after the match. Our coach had a puncture and came to a standstill. Two men in a lorry stopped and helped us. We offered them the Yugoslavian money that we had as a way of thanks. But they declined and asked if they could have some of the Welsh F.A. badges that we were wearing instead. Obviously we were more than happy to oblige and they went on their way as happy as Larry".

John, whose greatest footballing memories are of his time at Stoke and of the League Cup run itself, now lives quietly near the coast in South Wales. However, the name of Mahoney still lives on in the sporting arena, as one of his three daughters – Derrith – recently became the third generation Mahoney to represent her country. She follows her grandfather Joseph, who played Rugby League, Dad John who played Football, to play soccer for the national women's side. An achievement of which John is rightly proud! And so he should be.

The Other Squad Members.

There were five other players who played in the victorious League Cup run in 1971-72. They were; John Farmer, Sean Haslegrave, Willie Stevenson, Stuart Jump and Eric Skeels. Whilst they didn't take part in the final itself, their part in the earlier rounds of the competition were equally as important. This section of the book looks at their lives and careers.

This chapter has been kindly supported by Jeremy Paul.

Pic. courtesy of The Sentinel

John Farmer

Born in Biddulph, on 31st August 1947, John joined the 'Potters' in 1964 from the local league side Chatterley Boys Club. He made one appearance in the 1971-72 League Cup run.

Two years after joining Stoke City as a 16-year old he made his 1st team debut in January 1966 coming into the side to play against Arsenal. He quickly claimed the 'keepers shirt for his own. A player of undoubted talent, his career at Stoke was severely hindered when the club signed Gordon Banks (and much later Peter Shilton). This situation still rankles with the likeable Farmer who, even today, thinks that he was treated abysmally by the club's management. A view which has been echoed by many observers, including several of his former team-mates. As such he didn't want to assist with the either the researching or writing of this part of the book. Whilst he was with the club for 11 years he made only 185 first team appearances in total but never let the side down when he did actually play. He did manage to impress the, then, England manager Sir Alf Ramsey enough to be chosen for the England under 23 team that played against Wales in 1967.

John played against Southport in the first game of the successful League Cup run and was more than instrumental in keeping the side in the competition when he made a world class save that even the great Gordon Banks would have had problems saving. Despite this save and the level of his performance John was dropped, being replaced by Banks as soon as the England 'keeper was fully fit again.

Further to the 185 games that John played for Stoke he also represented West Bromwich Albion, guesting for the Staffordshire club during the ' Baggies' pre-season tour in 1972. Stoke also loaned him out to Leicester City during the 1973-74 season where he played twice for the 'Foxes'. He severed all ties with the club that he so loyally represented but whom treated him so abysmally in 1975 when he moved to Northwich Victoria. Today, John distances himself from the world of football. Instead he has found fame within another field, he has become a very successfully published poet.

14

Pic. E. Fuller

<u>Sean Haslegrave</u>

Born in Stoke-on-Trent on June 7th 1951, "Charlie Bubbles" signed for Stoke in 1968. A versatile player, who could play in midfield or as a striker, he played in two games and was on the substitutes bench for a third match of the League Cup run, scoring one goal.

'Charlie' another product of the City of Stoke-on-Trent schools system joined the Victoria Ground staff in November 1968. Like Stuart Jump, Sean was an important squad member who, following his debut against Derby County on December 26th 1970, went on to make more than 100 1st team appearances but never really established himself as a regular.

Sean played in the first two games of the League Cup run against Southport and Oxford United. However, Tony Waddington went with a more defensive midfield line-up for the 3rd round replay and he was relegated to the subs. bench. Sean replaced Greenhoff, who suffered from a groin strain, in the 65th minute. He made his mark on the game, with less than 5 minutes left, by scoring Stoke's second goal of the match. Unfortunately, he missed the latter rounds of the competition after receiving a cartilage injury, which required surgery to correct the problem.

Brian Clough came in and bought Sean for £35,000 in 1976 and Charlie duly became a Forest player. As with his time at Stoke he became a good squad player who, whilst on the fringe of a first team place, never really established himself there either.

Upon leaving the City Ground, Sean had spells with Preston North End and York City (where he came into contact with his former Stoke City team-mate Denis Smith). Denis recalls that " 'Bubble' was a true professional who led by example". Sean recalls that at that time Denis was eager for his players to get a better understanding of the game by getting coaching qualifications, so he enlisted on one such course and found that it was being taken by another of his old Stoke City team mates – Mike Pejic. Looking back at that time Sean laughs as he recalls: "Mike didn't do me any favours, if anything he made me work harder than all of the others. But it stood me in good stead as in my later career I have been able to coach some very good youngsters".

Following this he also had spells with Crewe Alexandra and a second spell at York before moving south to Torquay United. Moving back to the north of England he puts his coaching talents to good use working in the Footballing Academy at Preston that he helped to set up.

15

Pic. courtesy of The Sentinel

Willie Stevenson

Born on 26th October 1939, in Scotland, Willie joined Stoke in 1967 for a fee of £48,000, following a successful career with both Glasgow Rangers and Liverpool. A talented wing-half or centre-back, he was on the substitutes bench for the first game in the League Cup campaign and played in the second match at Oxford United's Manor Ground.

Willie entered the world of football as a 16-year old. However, because of his age he wasn't allowed to sign professionally for Glasgow Rangers, so he was farmed out to the 'Gers feeder club Dalkeith Thistle. Willie's talent was acknowledged by Rangers when, on his 17th birthday in 1956, they gave him a professional contract. He broke into their 1st team on 25th October 1958, the day before his 19th birthday, when manager Scott Symon selected him to play at wing-half. Willie remembers his debut very well, recalling:

"I made my debut against Stirling Albion, in a 2-2 draw and didn't look back. I kept my place for the rest of the season, playing 65 games in total. We were in the Glasgow Cup, the Charity Cup, the Scottish Cup, the Scottish League and the European Cup where we won through to the semi-final, only to be beaten by Eintract Frankfurt. (The German club went on to play the all-conquering Real Madrid in the final at Hampden Park and were soundly thrashed 7-3). I kept my place in the 1st team during the following season, playing behind Rangers new boy Jim Baxter in another 64 games for the club. Looking back, I feel that it was an awful lot of football for a young man. Indeed, whilst we won the Glasgow Cup, the Charity Cup, the Scottish League and the Scottish Cup, in reality there was too much pressure on me and I duly suffered the following year".

Willie freely admits that his form dipped during his third season with the Ibrox club. This dip in form resulted him being relegated to the reserve side for the remainder of that season. As his contract expired Willie was offered the chance of moving to Australia. However Rangers wouldn't allow him to play there as they still held his F.I.F.A. registration and were rather loath to release him from it. Despite the personal intervention of no less a personage as Stanley Rous, the then President of the world's governing body, Rangers dug their heels in and refused to release Willie ordered him to return to Glasgow.

A few months later, Willie moved south to Bill Shankly's Liverpool and embarked on another successful chapter of his footballing career. Playing alongside his international colleagues Tommy Lawrence, Ron Yeats and Ian St. John he became a member of a side that won the 1st Division Championship, the F.A. Cup (beating Leeds 2-1) and a second 1st Division title in consecutive seasons. However, Shanks was rebuilding a side that had aged together and had acquired the signature of the young Emlyn Hughes from Blackpool for £65,000. This meant that Willie was playing more and more Central League football. After half a season in the reserves Tony Waddington offered him a lifeline and, once City's offer of £48,000 was accepted, he duly became a Stoke player. "We had some fun during my time at Stoke, there was a blend of youth and experience and characters at the club. Players such as 'Taffy' (Roy Vernon),

Peter Dobing, Calvin Palmer and the nucleus of local lads such as Denis Smith, Mickey Pejic and Alan Bloor all gelled to create this friendly atmosphere. Allied to this was the way in which Tony Waddington managed the side. He encouraged the mix, as the experienced members of the squad passed on their expertise to the younger players".

Playing either in midfield or central defence Willie continued to contribute to the sides continued presence in the first division. By the 'semi-final' years Willie freely admits that his 1st team opportunities were getting rarer but he was involved in the early stages of the successful League Cup run of 1971-72 by being named as substitute against Southport before entering the fray, when Waddo named him in the starting line-up to face Oxford United at their Manor Ground. What does he recall of those two games? "I didn't come on at Southport but the game at Oxford was quite memorable. It had rained heavily and the pitch was muddy. Indeed the conditions prevented us from advancing into their half very often. However, we did get over their line and managed a draw. But when I see Oxford on T.V. nowadays and see the immaculate state of their pitch I can't help thinking back to the 4 inches of mud that we played in that night".

Willie's 1st team season came to an abrupt end two weeks later at 'Spurs when Steve Perryman broke his leg with an 'over the top' tackle that really should have brought about a sending-off for the young Londoner. Willie managed a couple of reserve games prior to the League Cup final itself but obviously wasn't fully match-fit. Looking back, Willie remembers the way in which Tony Waddington handled the situation saying; "Tony took me to one side the week before the game and said that he would have liked to have included me in the squad but he couldn't really take the chance on my fitness at Wembley. He did, however, keep those of us who weren't involved in the game in touch with the events of the day by having us on the bench, alongside him and the others".

A funny thing happened to Willie on the day of the final itself, as he recalls; "I had a very good friend, a little Irishman from Dublin named Seamus who was our unofficial lucky mascot. He followed us throughout the run and usually appeared in the most unusual of places. To my surprise, when we walked into the Wembley dressing-room we were welcomed by none other than Seamus. How he got there I'll never know but there he was. After the game had finished and the lap of honour had been completed we returned to the dressing-room and lo and behold there he was supping champagne with Tony and toasting each one of us as we walked in the room. He even made it to the reception at the Russell Hotel that night!"

After the final Willie spent the remainder of the season and much of the next year in the reserves before being given a 'free' at the end of that season. After a six month spell with Tranmere Rovers playing under his former Anfield and Scotland team-mate Ron Yeats, he joined Vancouver Whitecaps in the North American Soccer League on a two-year contract. However, during his second season in Canada Willie damaged the ligaments in his leg and was forced to retire.

Willie's opportunity on the international front were limited, but when looking back at that time it is not difficult to see why. He was challenging for the left-half shirt with the likes of the 'mighty' Dave Mackay and 'Slim' Jim Baxter. He won his first cap on Scotland's European tour in 1960 in the 2-2 draw in Holland. Like Terry Venables (with England), Willie has the distinction of representing his country at every level: - Schools and the Youth (both as captain), Under 23, Scottish League and Full International.

Having left the world of professional football Willie entered the licensed trade running his own public house until he retired. Today, he lives in South Cheshire and is a regular visitor to the Britannia Stadium where he casts a knowing eye over the proceedings on the pitch whilst catching up with all of his old team-mates.

16

Pic. E. Fuller

<u>Stuart Jump</u>

Born on January 27th 1952, in Crumpshall near Manchester, 'Jock' joined the Potters in August 1967. He played in five games during the League Cup run.

Stuart joined the apprentice staff at the Victoria Ground in August 1967 straight from school, as either a central-defender or defensive midfield player. Within two seasons the quiet, Lancashire lad had established himself as a 'regular' in the reserve side. First team chances proved to be scarce as the central defensive unit of Smith and Bloor were covered by Eric Skeels and Willie Stevenson. Whilst the defensive midfield slot was usually being contested for by Mickey Bernard and Josh Mahoney. Jock finally got his opportunity to play for the first team, making his debut on February 6th 1971 - against Coventry City at the Victoria Ground.

The following (League Cup) season saw Stuart making 30 1st team appearances, including 5 games in the run itself. He took over the central defensive role as Alan Bloor missed the game against Oxford. Bluto returned for the replay but Tony Waddington kept the young Mancunian in the side as he strengthened his midfield line-up. Stuart then realised two of his childhood ambitions in the 4th round tie against Manchester United. He played at Old Trafford against his boyhood hero's Manchester United and was given the task of marking his favourite player Denis Law. The former county schoolboy also marked Law in the replay at the Victoria Ground but missed out when Tony Waddington brought in Josh Mahoney for the 3rd game. His final appearance during that epic journey to the League Cup final was in the 1st leg of the semi-final where he partnered Alan Bloor at the centre of the defence, as Smithy was missing.

Always on the fringe of 1st team selection, Stuart never really made such an impression as to claim a regular position as his own and Waddo duly loaned him out to Malcolm Alison's Crystal Palace. He impressed the brash Londoner and the 'Eagles' boss contacted Waddo with the intention of making an offer for Stuart. Waddo would have released the young defender on a free but, as the story goes when Malcolm spoke to him on the 'phone, he said, "I am willing to offer £50,000 for Stuart". This totally blew Tony's mind and he spluttered "You what!" Alison mis-understood Waddington's reaction and said "alright I'll go as high as £70,000, but that's my final offer!" Tony Waddington agreed and Stuart left the Victoria Ground for the bright lights of London and Selhurst Park.

During the next 5 years Stuart made 80 appearances for Crystal Palace and was loaned out to Fulham on two separate occasions before moving to America. He joined the Tampa Bay Rowdies before playing for Houston Hurricane and then the Minnesota Kicks. During this time he was chosen to play for 'team' America during the Bicentennial tournament against England and Italy. Today, he still lives in North America but is an occasional visitor to North Staffordshire, visiting the friends that he made during his time with Stoke City.

17

Pic. E. Fuller

<u>Eric Skeels</u>

Born on 27th October 1939, in Eccles (Lancashire) 'Alfie' was the longest serving squad member who participated in the League Cup run. Having signed for the Potters in 1959, he missed most of the cup run because of injury. However, Waddo called him into the side that faced West Ham United in the 2nd leg of the semi-final and was on the 'bench' for the replay at Hillsboro'.

Alfie joined the Potters in 1959, having already had trials and offers from both Stockport County and Birmingham City, prior to being recommended to Frank Taylor at Stoke. Having played in a mid-week trial against West Bromwich Albion, in which he recalls:

"Jeff Astle (who later played for England and scored Albion's winning goal in the 1968 F.A. Cup final against Everton), played against me that day". Eric must have impressed, as he was asked to play in that season's F.A. Youth Cup, four weeks later. In between the trial and the Youth Cup game Eric played for Stoke's A team, becoming a regular in the junior ranks. He was offered a professional contract after the game against Wolves, Eric remembers:

"Tony (Waddington), who at that time was Frank Taylor's assistant manager, came up to me asking if I would be happy to sign for Stoke. I was and soon became a Stoke player".

By the 1962-63 season Eric was a 1st team regular during their challenge for the 2nd Division title. He has fond memories of that time, when he recalls: "We were surviving on gates of 7-8,000 and then Tony brought back Stanley Matthews from Blackpool. Then it all went crazy, we were getting gates of 35,000 and obviously the atmosphere at the Victoria Ground changed". Waddo also brought in a number of more experienced players: - Jimmy McIlroy, Jackie Mudie etc. who, along with Stan and Eric, won the 1962-63 2nd division title. Looking back at his career, Eric cites that season as being the one that provides his abiding footballing memory, as he recalls;

"After the Luton match, which we won, we went into the director's box to be presented to the crowd, who had run onto the pitch after the final whistle. It was an amazing feeling, as we looked down at all those fans we realised that we were 2nd Division Champions".

Known as 'Mr. Versatile' Eric played in every position for Stoke bar goalkeeper. "And I only missed that because I wasn't the tallest of players". However, continuing, he says: "Whilst I wore each shirt, once the match had kicked-off I would usually revert to my usual defensive role". Was being such a versatile player a draw back to his playing career? "To a certain extent it was and while I did play in other positions I was usually brought back into the defensive line-up of 'Waddington's Wall'". Looking back at this Eric remembers one Boxing Day match at Anfield. "Several of my friends had travelled to the game and as the announcer broadcast the Stoke team, he got to the number 9 shirt and said, 'number nine and centre-forward Eric Skeels'. Which brought about a certain amount of amusement to them".

Pic. E. Fuller

During the first season in division one, Stoke City won through to the two-legged League Cup Final, where they were to meet a Leicester City side that included Gordon Banks. The City side included Peter Dobing and John Ritchie as well as Eric. Leicester eventually ran out 4-3 winners. In the latter half of the 1960s, it may be fair to say that Eric's versatility did indeed hinder his career as several players broke into the side and established themselves in their own defensive right. But, ever the consummate professional, Eric was still an integral part of the 1st team squad and more than played his part during the F.A. Cup runs of 1970-71 and 1971-72.

In the 1970-71 season, Eric broke his leg in a game against Leicester City, as he recalls: "Steve Whitworth caught my leg in a tackle, but I continued to the end of the game out on the wing. It wasn't until the next day that we actually discovered that I had broken it. So I missed a lot of the season". Fortunately the defensive line-up of Marsh, Smith, Bloor and Pejic had become a 1st team fixture and apart from injury or suspension picked itself. But, by the second leg of the League Cup semi-final, Denis Smith was out through injury and Tony Waddington drafted Eric into the starting line-up. "Denis picked up an injury during the first leg of the semi-final at the Victoria Ground and as I had recovered from my broken leg I was called up into the squad. Waddo decided that Stuart Jump wasn't experienced enough to handle the pressure, so I partnered Bluto in the centre of the defence". Stoke won this exciting tie 1-0, drawing 2-2 on aggregate and a replay was required. "I was on the bench for the game at Hillsboro' as Denis had returned to reclaim his number 5 jersey, Tony wanted to strengthen the defence should we take an early lead". That was an end of Eric's playing involvement in the run itself as John Mahoney was chosen as substitute at Wembley. When did Eric find out that he wasn't to be a part of Stoke's biggest ever day? "Tony told me on the coach as we approached Wembley that Josh would be on the bench and while I didn't particularly like his decision I had to accept it. It was a great blow, after all I had been with the club for 13 years by then and had never set foot on Wembley. But that's football. There is only room for twelve players in the team and Tony's choice proved to be right as we won 2-1".

For the next 2 to 3 seasons Eric was in and out of the team, getting the occasional extended run when he played well. However, at the end of the 1976-77 season, Waddo told Eric that he was to be given a free-transfer. A decision which brought a 15-year playing career at Stoke to an end. His footballing days were far from over as he was invited to join Geoff Hurst in America to play for Seattle Sounders in the N.A.S.L. Eric played in the States for 6 months before returning to England, where he played for Port Vale until the end of the 1977-78 season.

After a life time in the professional ranks, Eric entered the licensed trade, running a pub in Glossop. At the same time he continued to be involved with football, regularly turning out for Leek Town. The call of the Potteries proved to be too great and Alfie returned 'home' to North Staffordshire where, for the past 12 years, he has been working at Staffordshire University's Stoke Campus. Today, he can still be seen at the Britannia Stadium, as he regularly attends the home games of his beloved Stoke City.

The Management

There were four other men who helped to shape the side that won the 1972 League Cup Final for Stoke City and, while they didn't physically perform on the pitch, their contribution was equally as important. They were the management team of Tony Waddington, Alan A'Court, Frank Mountford and Mike Allen. This section of the book pays tribute to them.

This chapter has been kindly supported by Bruce Green.

Tony Waddington (Manager):

"Waddo" as the likeable Mancunian was universally known, was the most successful manager that Stoke City has ever had. Born in Manchester on November 9th 1924, he joined the Potters coaching staff in 1952, after a playing career, with both Manchester United and Crewe Alexandra, had been foreshortened by a recurring knee injury. He was promoted - some four years later - to the position of assistant to manager Frank Taylor.

When Taylor was dismissed, in 1959, the club chose to promote from within and Waddo duly became 1st team manager. He inherited a side that for the previous few seasons had languished in the middle to lower regions of the 2nd division. As he attempted to build a side that would, eventually, challenge for the major honours he was shackled by an, almost, empty purse and became renowned for purchasing the services of players who were reaching the end of their playing careers. Players such as Jackie Mudie and Jimmy Mcilroy extended their careers by several seasons after signing for Stoke. However, his greatest acquisition was the purchase of the 46-year old Stanley Matthews, for the princely sum of £2,500. This amazing transfer boosted the club's gates from a paltry 8,409 to just under 35,000, thereby repaying the fee immediately. His faith in experience was more than repaid, in the 1962-63 season, as his side won the 2nd division championship, with the goal that clinched promotion being scored by none other than Stan Matthews himself.

Following their promotion to the 1st division, Waddo once again set about rebuilding his side, this time by combining experience with youthful exuberance. Once again he astounded the footballing community with another transfer coup when, in 1967, he paid the miserly sum of £52,000 for the services of the world's greatest goalkeeper – Gordon Banks. By August 1969 he had rebuilt his side into a team that would be challenging for football's major honours. Indeed there followed a purple patch in the club's history during which they reached two F.A.Cup semi-finals, won the League Cup, played in the UEFA cup two seasons running and finished 5th in the league in two consecutive years (1973-4 and 1974-75). He had also acquired several outstanding new players during this time, including Peter Shilton, Geoff Salmons and Alan Hudson.

Waddo's career at Stoke ended in 1977 when, following the collapse of the Butler Street Stand roof, he was forced to sell his best players just to balance the books! The enforced sale of the leading players weakened the side and, as the Potters lost their 1st division status, he resigned. Tony returned to the game in 1979, taking up the reins at his old club Crewe. Leaving there in 1981, he severed all connections with the world of football until 1993 when he was appointed to the board of Stoke City as an associate director. He remained in this role until his death in January 1994.

Alan A'Court (Coach);

"Ackers", the former Liverpool and England wing-half joined the coaching staff at the Victoria Ground in 1971. A likeable man, he soon settled in the area and was an integral part of the coaching set-up with Stoke City during their 'glory years' in the early part of the 1970s. He, initially, continued his role as 1st team coach under George Eastham after Waddo left the club until Skippy departed in 1978, when he took over as caretaker-manager until the appointment of Alan Durban in February of that year. Following stints at Crewe Alexandra (as manager-coach) and Chester, as assistant-manager, he left the world of football and took up the position of manager of the Sir Stanley Matthews sports centre at Staffordshire University. A position he held until he retired recently.

Frank Mountford (Coach);

This quiet pipe-smoker from North Yorkshire first joined the Potters in 1937. He signed professional forms during World War Two and having broken into the 1st team, became a regular for much of the following 13 years. Remembered, fondly, as a 'classy' wing-half he finally retired from the game – after playing over 600 1st team matches – in 1958. Following his retirement, he continued his association with the side for the next 20 years, initially as the club trainer until physio. Fred Street joined Stoke, then as 1st team coach – continuing his association with the club until the appointment of Alan Durban. Today, this much-admired man still lives – in peaceful retirement – on the outskirts of Stoke-on-Trent.

Mike Allen (Physio.);

Mike, a former RAF man, joined the backroom staff at the Victoria Ground when Fred Street left to take up similar duties with the Arsenal. He combined his 1st team duties with his private practice in Newcastle. He left the Victoria Ground in the mid 1980s to concentrate all his energies into his ever-developing practice. The abiding memory that most Stoke fans will have of him during the final would be as he and Jack Marsh scrabbled about on the Wembley pitch searching for Jackie's missing Contact lens.

Our Opponents

There were two teams at Wembley that day and while we are paying tribute to the winning side we must not forget Chelsea's contribution to the final. With that in mind, this section of the book looks at our opponents through the eyes of a player who later became a legend at the Victoria Ground and who willingly gave his time freely to talk about the League Cup final of 1972 – Alan Hudson.

This chapter has been kindly supported on behalf of Carole - the original Golden Goal Girl.

Our Opponents

A Wembley cup final is about winners and losers, as it should be. But when recalling the occasion on which the so-called 'underdogs' succeeded, we should not erase from our memory the fact that there was indeed another team at the national stadium on that momentous day. Indeed, the popular press had suggested that all the 'Kings' of the Kings Road had to do on 4th March was to turn at Wembley and the League Cup would be as good as theirs, by totally dismissing the chances of Waddington's Warriors. Did this added pressure have any great effect upon the Chelsea players? To answer this and other questions I have gone into the enemy camp and met up with the former Chelsea midfielder Alan Hudson!

"When you look back at the video of the day you can see a difference between the two sets of players from the start. As we lined-up in the tunnel, the Stoke players looked relaxed, almost as though they were just going out for a training session, whilst we looked tense. Thinking back to that day I cannot really remember why we were like that because the atmosphere in the dressing-room was no different to that of a 'normal' league game. However, subconsciously we may have been dwelling upon the results of our last two games prior to the final. After all, the previous Saturday we had been knocked out of the F.A. Cup by Leyton Orient and in the midweek we went out of the European Cup-Winners Cup. So the thought of losing in a third cup competition within the same week probably did weigh upon our minds a little".

"On the other hand we may have been a little over confident because I think that we were all very surprised to be playing Stoke. When we saw the draw for the semi-finals being made, we felt that it was a reasonable bet that it would probably be an all-London final, as we faced Spurs in one game whilst Stoke, as we all know, played that mammoth tie against West Ham".

The result of the tie against the 'Hammers' is well known to all Stoke fans but what about the other semi-final, obviously Chelsea won but was it as exciting as our game? Huddy replies; "I think it was, but whilst we didn't have to play any extra games, it was an epic and exciting game in its own right that, like the Stoke - West Ham tie, would have been worthy of the final itself. Obviously we won and I was fortunate enough to score one of the two goals that got us to the final – the 'sponge' Tommy Baldwin got the other and so we faced our third cup final in three years".

On, then, to the final itself and the Chelsea team that played in it. What are Alan's thoughts about his colleagues who lined up against Stoke City that day? Looking back, he goes through the team and describes each as follows: -

Peter Bonetti.

" 'The cat'. 'Catty' was probably the second best goalkeeper in the country, if not the world, in those days. Obviously Gordon – the world's greatest – played for Stoke. Peter was an agile and athletic 'keeper who was a 'confidence' player and, to be honest, I felt that the way in which the media blamed him for the World Cup defeat in Mexico didn't help at all. Unlike a lot of the squad he was a quiet and unassuming guy who just got on with the job – but on his day he was unbeatable".

Paddy Mulligan.

"Paddy was a rarity! An Irishman who was teetotal. I think that he was a much under-rated player and whilst not in the defensive/attacking style of either Jackie or Pej. he was a solid capable defender. He must have been good, as he managed to keep Eddie McCreadie out of the team".

John Dempsey.

"The quiet man of the team. John joined Chelsea from Fulham and quickly established himself as a more than capable defender – who, like Paddy Mulligan and T.C., represented the Republic of Ireland. He made his debut for Chelsea on the same day as I did. Physically he was very similar in build to Denis Smith and whilst not quite as robust as Smithy – on his day – was almost impossible to get past".

David Webb.

" 'Big' Dave was the 'character' and 'comedian' of the side. His playing style was a combination of both Smithy and Bluto in as much as he was uncompromising. Another 'confidence' player, he will forever be remembered by the Chelsea faithful for the goal he scored in the F.A. Cup final replay in 1970 at Old Trafford which won us the cup against Leeds".

Ron Harris (Captain).

" 'Chopper' led by example. He would run through a wall for the Chelsea cause. People think he got the nick-name because of his tackling ability but in reality it was because of his 'tackle' ". (laughs).

Charlie Cooke

"A wizard of the wing, Charlie was one of our players who could turn a game on its head in a second. However, at that time he had a drink problem and I think that it had a serious, detrimental effect on his playing ability. He was similar in style to T.C. but wasn't quite confident enough to wander all over the pitch like Terry did".

John Hollins.

"A little midfield dynamo, similar to Bernie or Josh. John had an exceptionally long throw for such a small man. I felt that he was another much under-rated player who should have gained more international honours than he did".

Alan Hudson.

"Me! I remember early in the game trying to make a pass and ballooning the ball into the air. I looked up to the heavens and thought 'this isn't going to be my day' I didn't perform half as well as I knew I could have, as I made my 1st Wembley appearance. I was also at fault for the winning Stoke goal as it was me who should have been marking George Eastham. When the cross came in and Jimmy Greenhoff hit it, I thought that 'Catty' would save it easily. So I moved away expecting a quick throw out – but we all know what happened don't we?"

Peter Houseman.

"Peter, who unfortunately, alongside his wife, died in a car crash several seasons after the final, was another quite man of the team. Another non-drinker he never reached his full potential at the club and never really won the fans over on to his side".

Chris Garland.

"The blonde bombshell who joined us from Bristol City for £100,00 was a very quick player who nearly got the equaliser in the last few minutes of the game after latching onto Mickey Bernard's back-pass. He didn't get enough 1st team matches under his belt as Ian Hutchinson was Ossie's regular strike partner. However, when he did get into the side he never let us down".

Peter Osgood.

"Ossie was a striker who, with no disrespect to Reg, should have moved to Stoke with me. There is no doubt in my mind that if he had moved to the Victoria Ground we (Stoke) would have won the 1st division title. However, being a home-bird, he chose to stay in the south and moved to the Dell with Southampton instead. He was an amazing striker who could score goals with both feet as well as his head. He was a supremely confident, brave player who liked his (more than occasional) drink. His bravery was evident during the F.A. Cup final victory over Leeds United when he scored with a diving header, ignoring the flying boots of the Leeds defenders. One story does come to mind that, demonstrates both his drinking habits and the complete faith that he had in himself, occurred when we won the European Cup-Winners Cup Final in Vienna. The final was drawn and we needed a replay to decide the outcome. It was played two days later in Vienna, so we stopped in the city prior to the game. I was walking around the pool on the Thursday and saw Ossie having a drink with a couple of girls and several Chelsea fans in tow. When he saw me looking at him he smiled and said 'don't worry, you just get the ball to me tomorrow and I'll get a goal'. The following day he duly obliged and won the game for us".

Tommy Baldwin.

"The 'sponge' as he is known to us. Not only because he would soak up the pressure on the pitch but also because of the amount that he would drink, was another player who didn't get the recognition that he deserved. He played second fiddle to Hutch (Ian Hutchinson) so had limited opportunities to shine. I don't think that he had much chance of making an impression on the final because when he finally got onto the pitch he had to play out of position".

"I don't think that we played as well that day as we should have but that shouldn't take anything away from the way which Stoke performed. Indeed, they really did deserve to win on that occasion". After the match Chelsea (like Stoke) had a celebration in London but Alan wasn't up for it and walked into the cold night air to get away from the crowds. Dave Sexton joined him and said: "Don't let it get you down, you have a great future here and will soon be the captain". But this didn't happen as in 1974 Alan left London and moved north to join us here at The Victoria Ground.

Huddy was an instant success and the Boothen-enders took the talented midfielder to their hearts. Likewise, the likeable Londoner took the Potteries to his heart and built a rapport that lasts to this day. He recalls his time with Stoke well when disclosing several little anecdotes about his team-mates and the 'Governor' Tony Waddington, saying: "I met Tony in London's Russell Square under the cloak of darkness to discuss my move to Stoke, it looked like a scene from a Harry Palmer film as we discussed terms and things. I arrived on the Monday and, booking into the North Stafford Hotel, I received a message to meet my new team-mates at The Place that night! The following day I met them officially at training. My other abiding memory of Tony was when we had lunch with my parents when they visited Stoke. He took us for a meal at Federation House and after lunch Waddo and my dad fell deep into conversation, whilst my mum and I went into the lounge. It was like looking at my two fathers together and that's how I felt about him – he was like a second father".

Alan left the Potters and following a brief spell with Arsenal, joined Jimmy Gabriel's Seattle Sounders in the N.A.S.L. Returning home he languished in the Chelsea reserve side before he got an urgent call from Waddo asking him to come back to Stoke as they battled against relegation. He did so and on the last day of the season they duly avoided the drop.

Today, following a serious accident and many operations, Alan is on the road to recovery. After a glittering career, that included several England caps, he was asked what his greatest footballing memory was. Smiling, he replied: "I had a dodgy ankle and wasn't sure that I would be fit enough to play for Stoke against Liverpool. However, Tony duly pulled one of his masterstrokes by getting the fire brigade in to water the pitch. The following day the Liverpool team arrived and were greeted by a pitch that resembled a quagmire. We beat them soundly and after the game, as we threw our muddy kit onto a pile in the centre of the floor, there was a knock at the dressing-room door. Bill Shankly stood there and asked if he could come in. Tony duly invited him in and Shanks entered. Looking around he spied me and asked if he could speak to me. The boss said that he could and Bill Shankly looked at me and said; "I have seen many great performances (including my hero Peter Doherty) during my years in football but what I witnessed today, as I watched you, was the greatest ever". Coming from Shanks that was praise indeed and is a sentiment that is echoed by the Potters faithful – who have a special place in their hearts for a man who played against us on Saturday 4th March 1972!

Appendix

League Cup 2nd Round: Southport v. Stoke City. Wednesday 8th September 1971.
Haig Avenue Southport. Attendance 10,223
Southport 1 Stoke City 2
Dunleavey. Bloor,
Greenhoff

Teams:

Southport: Taylor, Turner, Sibbald, McPhee, Dunleavey, Peat, Lee, Hartland,
Redrobe, Field, Hartle. sub. Lloyd.

Stoke City: Farmer, Marsh Pejic, Bernard, Smith, Bloor, Mahoney, Greenhoff,
Ritchie, Dobing, Haslegrave. sub. Stevenson.

League Cup 3rd Round;Oxford United v. Stoke City. Wednesday 6th October 1971.
Manor Ground Oxford.   Attendance 15,024
Oxford United 1 Stoke City 1
Evanson   Greenhoff

Teams:

Oxford United: Kearns, Way, Shuker, Roberts, C.Clarke, Evanson, Sloan, Skeen,
Clayton, Cassidy, Atkinson. sub. D.Clarke.

Stoke City: Banks, Marsh, Pejic, Bernard, Smith, Jump, Conroy, Greenhoff, Ritchie,
Stevenson, Haslegrave. sub. Mahoney.

League Cup 3rd Round replay: Stoke City v. Oxford United.
Monday 18th October 1971.
Victoria Ground Stoke on Trent.   Attendance 11,767
Stoke City 2 Oxford United 0
Ritchie
Haslegrave

Teams:

Stoke City: Banks, Marsh, Pejic, Bernard, Smith, Bloor, Conroy, Greenhoff, Ritchie,
Dobing, Jump. sub. Haslegrave.

Oxford United: Kearns, Lucas, Shuker, Roberts, C.Clarke, Evanson, Sloan,
G.Atkinson, Clayton, D.Clarke, Aylott. sub. Skeen.

League Cup 4th Round: Manchester United v. Stoke City.
                                  Wednesday 27th October 1971.
                                  Old Trafford Manchester   Attendance 47,062
                                  Manchester United 1 Stoke City 1
                                  Gowling   Ritchie

Teams:

Manchester United: Stepney, O'Neil, Burns, Gowling, James, Sadler, Morgan, Kidd,
                   Charlton, Law, Best. sub. Aston.

Stoke City: Banks, Marsh, Pejic, Bernard, Smith, Bloor, Conroy, Greenhoff,
                   Ritchie, Mahoney, Jump. sub. Eastham.

League Cup 4th Round replay: Stoke City v. Manchester United.
                                        Monday 8th November 1971.
                                        Victoria Ground Stoke on Trent.   Attendance 40,829
                                        Stoke City 0 Manchester United 0

Teams:

Stoke City: Banks, Marsh, Pejic, Bernard, Bloor, Jump, Conroy, Greenhoff,
                   Ritchie, Dobing, Mahoney. sub. Eastham.

Manchester United: Stepney, O'Neil, Burns, Gowling, James, Sadler, Morgan, Kidd,
                   Charlton, McIlroy, Best. sub. Aston.

League Cup 4th Round 2nd replay: Stoke City v. Manchester United
                                        Monday 15th November 1971.
                                        Victoria Ground Stoke on Trent.   Attendance 42,223
                                        Stoke City 2 Manchester United 1
                                        Dobing,   Best.
                                        Ritchie.

Teams:

Stoke City: Banks, Marsh, Pejic, Bernard, Smith, Bloor, Conroy, Greenhoff,
                   Ritchie, Dobing, Mahoney. sub. Eastham.

Manchester United: Stepney, O'Neil, Burns, Gowling, James, Sadler, Morgan,
                   McIlroy, Charlton, Sartori, Best. sub. Crerand.

172

League Cup 5th Round: Bristol Rovers v. Stoke City. Tuesday 23rd November 1971.
Eastville Stadium, Bristol.   Attendance 33,624
Bristol Rovers 2 Stoke City 4
Stubbs,   Greenhoff, .
Godfrey.   Smith,
                 Bernard,
                 Conroy

Teams:

Bristol Rovers: Sheppard, Roberts, Parsons, Godfrey, Taylor, Prince, Stephens,
                W.Jones, R.Jones, Stubbs, Jarman. sub. Allan.

Stoke City: Banks, Marsh, Pejic, Bernard, Smith, Bloor, Conroy, Greenhoff, Ritchie,
                Dobing, Eastham. sub. Mahoney.

League Cup Semi-final 1st leg: Stoke City v. West Ham United.
Wednesday 8th December 1971.
Victoria Ground Stoke on Trent   Attendance 36,400
Stoke City 1   West Ham United 2
Dobing   Hurst (pen)
               Best.

Teams:

Stoke City: Banks, Marsh, Pejic, Bernard, Bloor, Jump, Conroy, Greenhoff,
                Ritchie, Dobing, Eastham. sub. Mahoney.

West Ham United: Ferguson, McDowell, Lampard, Bonds, Taylor, Moore, Redknapp,
                Best, Hurst, Brooking, Robson. sub. Howe.

League Cup Semi-final 2nd leg: West Ham United v. Stoke City.
Wednesday 15th December 1971.
Upton Park West Ham.   Attendance 38,771
West Ham United 0 Stoke City 1
                         Ritchie.

Teams:

West Ham United: Ferguson, McDowell, Lampard, Bonds, Taylor, Moore, Redknapp,
                Best, Hurst, Brooking, Robson. sub. Howe.

Stoke City: Banks, Marsh, Pejic, Bernard, Bloor, Skeels, Conroy, Greenhoff,
                Ritchie, Dobing, Eastham. sub. Mahoney.

League Cup Semi-final replay: Stoke City v. West Ham United.
Wednesday 5th January 1972.
Hillsborough Sheffield   Attendance 46,916
Stoke City 0 West Ham United 0

Teams:

Stoke City: Banks, Marsh, Pejic, Bernard, Smith, Bloor, Conroy, Greenhoff,
                   Ritchie, Dobing, Eastham. sub. Skeels.

West Ham United: Ferguson, McDowell, Lampard, Bonds, Taylor, Moore, Redknapp,
                 Brooking, Hurst, Best, Robson. sub. Howe.

League Cup Semi-final 2nd replay: Stoke City v. West Ham United.
Wednesday   26th January 1972.
Old Trafford Manchester.   Attendance 49,247
Stoke City 3   West Ham United 2
Bernard,   Bonds,
Dobing,   Brooking.
Conroy.

Teams:

Stoke City: Banks, Marsh, Pejic, Bernard, Smith, Bloor, Conroy, Greenhoff,
                   Ritchie, Dobing, Eastham. sub. Mahoney.

West Ham United: Ferguson, McDowell, Lampard, Bonds, Taylor, Moore, Redknapp,
                 Best, Brooking, Robson. sub. Eustace.

League Cup Final: Stoke City v. Chelsea. Saturday 4th March 1972.
Wembley Stadium London   Attendance 100,000
Stoke City 2 Chelsea 1
Conroy,   Osgood.
Eastham.

Teams:

Stoke City: Banks, Marsh, Pejic, Bernard, Smith, Bloor, Conroy, Greenhoff, Ritchie,
            Dobing, Eastham. sub. Mahoney.

Chelsea: Bonetti, Mulligan, Harris, Hollins, Dempsey, Webb, Cooke, Garland,
                Osgood, Hudson, Houseman. sub. Baldwin.

Acknowledgements

As with any book of this genre, there are many people to thank and acknowledge.

I do so with the greatest humility and appreciation of their help and support. They are:

Those players of the 1972 League Cup squad who allowed me to invade their privacy and let me to take up their time.

Alec Bohannan, of Speciality Sports, for suggesting the book in the first instance.

Jo Bohannan, (the token Port Vale fan) for all the hours of proof reading.

Pamela Zeferino, for her patience when teaching me how to get the best out of my p.c. and assistance with proof reading.

Sean Dooley, Pam Young, Owen Ryles, Martin Spink, Hannah Crush and Stuart Robinson of the Sentinel, for all their help and support during my research and the writing of this book and for the donation of many of the photographs that have been used in this book.

Eddie Fuller, For the donation of many photographs in this book.

Ted Doe, for kindling my interest in Stoke City all those years ago.

And last but not least – my family;
Peggy Wood and Geoffrey Hine for their patience, understanding and support during the time that I have been working on this project.

<u>Sponsors</u>

We would like to thank the following people for their kind support of this book: -

Carl W. Holness

Roger Martin

Nick Hancock

Alec and Jo Bohannan

Phil Rawlins

Pamela Zeferino

Alan Peake

Jeremy Paul

Bruce Green

Eddie Fuller

The Sentinel